THE
ANGEL COMPANION

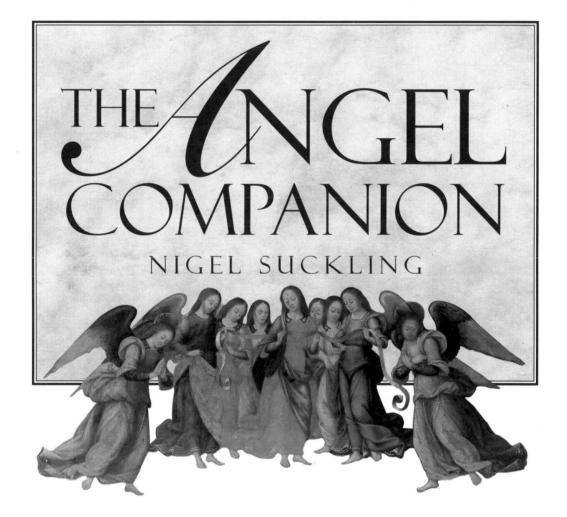

THE ANGEL COMPANION

NIGEL SUCKLING

BARNES
&NOBLE
BOOKS
NEW YORK

To Caryl, for everything
N.S.

This edition published by Barnes & Noble Inc.,
by arrangement with Pavilion Books Limited

2001 Barnes & Noble Books

M10 9 8 7 6 5 4 3 2 1

ISBN 0-7607-2706-6

First published in Great Britain in 2001 by
Pavilion Books Limited

Designed by Bernard Higton

Set in Berkeley Old Style Book
Colour origination by First Impressions
Printed and bound in Singapore by Imago

CONTENTS

INTRODUCTION

Angels are mysterious beings. They come into just about every second love song and we're surrounded by images of them at Christmas, but most of us really have only the vaguest idea of what angels are. This is not just a modern post-Christian understanding, since it has almost always been the case. Even at the height of their confidence most Christian authorities have had a bit of a problem with angels. They could not be ignored, but they also raised a few tricky theological questions. So most churches have discouraged too much curiosity about angels, taking their lead from St Paul, who famously warned against too many dealings with them because of the danger of being deceived by Satan's lot.

Jesus on the other hand had no such reservations, which says something about the difference between them. Thanks to the glowing accounts of angels in the Gospels they could not be banished entirely from the cosmological picture, but they were pushed as far as possible to the margins and St Paul was quoted when people asked too many questions. People were encouraged to relate to their personal guardian angel, but that was about it. They were allowed to know the names of archangels actually mentioned in the Bible, but wanting to know more was frowned upon.

Luckily some people have always ignored this disapproval and there has always been a lively underground tradition about angels within Christianity, as in Islam and Judaism. In fact, ideas about angels have always circulated freely between the three cultures with none of their usual theological bickering. This is a characteristic of angels themselves: they seem able to transcend the usual boundaries.

These days angels are enjoying quite a revival. As Westerners increasingly stay away from church in droves, there is a compensating growth of interest in angels, perhaps because they have always stood slightly outside organized religion and dogma. Agnostics, evangelical Christians and New Agers alike are showing new interest. As for the rest, Christmas may be the only time we decorate our homes with angels, but it is not all that unusual to find paintings or statues of them in the homes of atheists. Their images still conjure an aspiration to spirituality that most of us harbour, even if only as a wistful regret.

The old notion that we each have a good angel on one shoulder and a devil on the other still has resonance. That's often still how life feels. However much we claim to be the masters of our own destinies, there come times when it feels like someone behind the scenes is pulling strings. Our temptations and inspirations often still feel as if they come to us from outside of ourselves.

What is interesting about the emerging New Age vision of angels is that it rubs shoulders quite comfortably with a revived paganism. The parallels are suddenly more obvious between angels and, say, the elvish *Tuatha de Dannann* of Ireland, who are said to have come to earth in flying ships, creating order with God-like powers. In a way, angels are proving to be a bridge between Christianity and other mythologies. Many people find it quite easy to take on board the idea of them without having the faintest inclination to then go and join a church.

So angels are quite unusual in their range of appeal, but where do our ideas about them come from? Almost the least useful place to look is the Bible, where angels are mentioned often enough but with virtually no detail or background. Even the famous

legend of Satan being thrown out of heaven is only mentioned indirectly. Jewish tradition has much more to say, and is of course the fountain of all angelic lore. There are also countless wild mystical speculations about angels that have always flourished on the fringes of conventional belief. Between them all, something like a consistent picture has emerged. Some ideas have stuck, for whatever reason, and been absorbed into the tradition, and these are the ones which I will concentrate on in this book.

CHAPTER ONE

CHERUBS AND PUTTI

These truants from home and from Heaven,
They have made me more manly and mild;
And I know now how Jesus could liken
The Kingdom of God to a child.

CHARLES MONROE DICKINSON, *THE CHILDREN*

ngels come in all shapes and sizes. Some are austere and complex beings, powerful beyond our understanding and in tune with the most secret impulses of the universe. Others are comforting messengers with kind words of counsel, who we turn to in our moments of despair. Some are fallen angels that tempt us catastrophically astray, while some express the very simplest of virtues, such as innocence – the pure joy of life at its carefree beginning.

These are the cherubs that frolic around the margins of heavenly dramas like children at a wedding, reminding us that joy is more precious than gold, or half the things for which we struggle. Eternally young and uncluttered in their view, cherubs are the spirits of playfulness, bringing a human touch to paradise and a glimpse of paradise to earth.

Cherubs are now seen as little winged babies, but the word cherubim originally meant something very different. In the Bible cherubim are the awesome enforcers of divine law. They belong to the highest orders of angels, those farthest removed from the earthly sphere and therefore most alien to us. It was cherubim who guarded the gates of Eden with flaming swords against Adam and Eve's return (Genesis 3.24); and it was riding on the back of a cherub that God descended from heaven amid thunder, lightning, earthquake and flood to rescue David (2 Samuel 22.11; Psalm 18.10). The little cherubs we think of are at the opposite end of the angelic spectrum – sweet, innocent and playful. They bring a smile to our lips and lift our hearts.

So he drove out the man; and he placed at the east of the garden of Eden Cherubim, and a flaming sword which turned every way, to keep the way of the tree of life.

GENESIS 3

Although cherubs have long been accepted playing around the margins of religious art, theologians have never really settled their place in the angelic hierarchy. Almost none has ever claimed that they are babies in the sense that they will one day grow up to be archangels. They are eternally young, so it is widely believed they are the souls of children who die young, or maybe the souls of humans waiting to be born.

The idea that angels can become human (and vice versa) has always been popular though, especially in songs and folk belief. Some Church Fathers like Origen and various early Christian sects also believed it. Francis Barrett in his famous book *The Magus* (1801) listed Innocents (cherubs), Martyrs and Confessors (saints) as three additional ranks of angel below the nine accepted tiers. Swedenbourg went further and claimed to have been told by angels themselves that they all begin life as humans, whose destiny it is to evolve through the angelic hierarchy to merge eventually with the Godhead.

The purpose of the
creation of the universe is
an angelic heaven from the human race.

EMMANUEL SWEDENBOURG, *DIVINE LOVE AND WISDOM*, CHAPTER 3

*O*nce a dream did weave a shade
O'er my angel-guarded bed.

WILLIAM BLAKE, *SONGS OF INNOCENCE*

Indirectly, through William Blake and others, Swedenbourg's ideas have had a vast and largely unrecognized influence on Western thinking. Most other philosophers, though, have agreed that angels and humans are totally separate orders of being, and remain distinct even when inhabiting the same heaven.

So there is no real official sanction for the existence of sweet little cherubs in heaven and no clear view as to their nature, whether they are human souls or otherwise. In the end they seem to be in a class of their own, as with the Watchers (or Grigori) that we find in Genesis and *The Book of Enoch*. But official or not, sweet little cherubs are essential to Christian iconography, spontaneously created by artists and accepted simply because they seem right.

Cherubs first appeared as little winged babies (or sometimes just winged babies' heads) in Western paintings after the eighth century, when the Nicene Council decided to allow saints and angels to appear in religious art, which meant most art in those days. Also known as 'putti', which simply means 'little boys', they were modelled on the winged cupidons of classical Greece and Rome and thus were a subliminal link with all that was brightest in the pagan past, conjuring echoes of Eros and Aphrodite and playful, innocent sensuality. They provided an unconscious counterpoint to the solemn mysteries of the Church, a humanizing touch to its often killjoy morality.

Many people enjoy angels in art, particularly at Christmas, but feel unable to take them any more seriously than Santa Claus without also taking on religious baggage. Angels are certainly rooted in the Bible, Koran and Torah, but many people without any formal religion seem able not only to enjoy angels aesthetically but to feel them as a daily presence in their lives without any sense of contradiction. It seems increasingly possible to believe in angels as envoys from a spiritual realm, without having any fixed ideas about that place.

Even simply as colourful metaphors, angels and demons continue to play a large part in our imaginative lives. We all sometimes think 'The devil's in him (or her) today.' Or we might say 'Be an angel...' Some believe that the people who most irritate us are angels in disguise because they force us to confront our limitations.

In practice, everyone occasionally has to choose between their best and worst selves and it takes just a small step of the imagination to perceive this in the familiar terms of angels and devils. In a way, why not let our best impulses assume the sweet, beautiful and glorious forms angels have evolved over millennia? Why not let our ideals or guiding principles assume the wings and shining form of guardian angels so that we can relate to them as the living, autonomous entities they so often seem to be?

Perhaps much of the revival in angels' popularity, as we begin the third millennium, is because many of us do feel their continued presence, whether or not we go to church. In this, we have good company in Socrates, a stout atheist if ever there was one. He didn't believe in heaven but was convinced that everyone has a personal daemon, a kind of higher self that dictates their actions and the course of their life, and who is in the end, the final arbiter of whether that life is a success or a failure.

What we're interested in here is where the ideas about angels come from. Curiously enough, the Bible does not shed much light on the matter. Angels appear often enough, and even more in the New Testament than the Old, but remarkably few details are given away. They are at the heart of the drama but it is assumed the reader already knows who Michael, Gabriel and Raphael are, and how the powers, principalities and other ranks of angels are related. This was in fact the case when the scriptures were written, since it was quite common knowledge that the different orders of angels were distributed among the seven heavens. Therefore, the prophets and apostles felt no need to go into detail.

In the cradle of Christianity there were many sources of angelic lore that once carried the same weight of authority as the books of the Bible, but were later almost forgotten. Chief of them was *The Book of Enoch*, which is often quoted in the New Testament both directly and indirectly, and whose mood in fact permeates the whole teaching far more than anything from the Old Testament.

The Book of Enoch was left out of the Bible but a century or two later was still being quoted by Church Fathers such as Irenaeus, Clement of Alexandria and Tertullian, with as much confidence as if it was Genesis. How it came to be excluded and then completely lost is an interesting saga in itself, but its rediscovery in Ethiopia in the eighteenth century was like finding the lost pieces of a jigsaw. Suddenly many untraceable scriptural quotes found their home, as did many ideas of early Christianity that had been assumed to come from direct revelation.

Enoch was one of the main sources of Christian angel lore. The other was the *De Coelesti Hierarchia*, or Hierarchies of Heaven. This was supposed to have been written by Dionysius the Areopagite, Paul's famous convert on the Hill of Mars in Athens (Acts

The angels' ... task is to act as intermediaries, handing on to us whatever
God has decided, just as superior angels have handed these on to them.

PSEUDO-DIONYSIUS, *LETTER TO DEMOPHILUS*

Every angel is a heaven in miniature.
EMMANUEL SWEDENBOURG, *DIVINE LOVE AND WISDOM*

17). Because of this, it was treated almost as gospel for centuries, but it also carried weight simply because it crystallized the prevailing beliefs clearly and systematically.

Dionysius' book had enormous influence in the Middle Ages through a translation by John the Scot in the ninth century. This is the philosopher who, one night as they were quaffing wine, was asked by King Charles the Bald: 'What's the difference between a Scot and a sot?' Quick as a flash John replied 'The width of this table' and rather luckily lived to tell the tale.

Despite the author proving to be someone else entirely who lived about five hundred years after St Paul, Dionysius' hierarchy of angels remains the official teaching of the Catholic Church today. This is largely thanks to its adoption by St Thomas Aquinas as the basis of his own angel lore in the *Summa Theologica*, which remains a cornerstone of Catholic belief.

The poet Dante (1265–1321) also adopted Dionysius' scheme for his description of heaven in *The Divine Comedy*. In 'Paradise' (canto 28) he has it explained by his muse, the saintly Beatrice, who concludes with a nod of gratitude:

Now Dionysius set himself of old
To contemplate these orders with such zeal,
That he assigned to them the names I gave.

So being proved a forgery in fact did the book's influence little harm. The mentality behind such 'pious forgeries' is now obscure but it's worth remembering that it has also been shown that many New Testament writings date from long after the event and cannot be by the claimed authors. The same goes for many Old Testament books such as Daniel. Who wrote them is, in the end, less important than what they say and whether they are believed.

Dionysius, or Pseudo-Dionysius as he became known, laced his treatise heavily with scriptural quotes, but the basic scheme came from elsewhere and owes much to Greek philosophy. He divided angels into nine orders or choirs grouped in three triads or trinities. This was a favourite neo-Platonic device in which the middle unit is seen as combining the extremes on either side to form a unified whole.

According to this scheme the triad furthest removed from us and closest to the Divine Source consists of seraphim, cherubim and ophanim. The middle triad consists of dominations, virtues and powers; and the third of principalities, archangels and angels. It is from the last tier that our guardian angels are drawn.

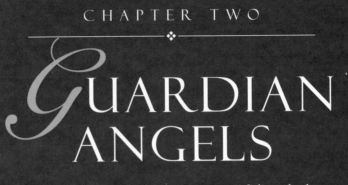

Guardian angels are drawn from the first rank (from our point of view) in Dionysius' celestial hierarchy. He calls them simply 'angels' which is a bit confusing because all the others are also called angels at times. His explanation is that all are angels in one sense, but some have special powers and duties that give them other titles as well.

Guardian angels are the least of the heavenly powers, but they are also the most familiar and so colour our perceptions of the others, who often defy description. Guardian angels are the closest to us by nature and share many of our concerns. Their heavenly sphere adjoins and even overlaps our material world. Visitors to their realm have been dazzled by its seeming perfection and ethereal beauty, but the angels say that the higher realms are more dazzling still, each level of heaven being progressively less material and more full of light than the one before. So, to our eyes, the sphere of guardian angels seems dazzling perfection, but that is how they view the next heaven, where their own guardians dwell.

Guardian angels are our personal ambassadors to the Divine. Some Christians imagine that people acquire them through baptism, but most agree that everyone has a guardian angel whatever they believe in, and however virtuous or not they are. Whether our angel comes at birth or conception is about the only real point of argument. Some say that a baby is looked after by its mother's guardian angel before birth and only then acquires its own. Others believe this happens at conception and that for the next nine months the baby's soul is cared for in heaven, one of the explanations for *putti* we met earlier. But either way, pagans and Christians alike are supposed to have at least one guardian angel from birth.

I Dreamed a Dream! What can it mean?
And that I was a maiden Queen
Guarded by an Angel mild:
Witless woe was ne'er beguiled!

WILLIAM BLAKE, SONGS OF EXPERIENCE

SOURCES

Believers in this often quote the above saying from Matthew's Gospel, because of course the children Jesus was talking about were unbaptized Jews. It was also Old Testament belief that every nation had its guardian angel, or principality, even those that gave the Israelites a hard time such as the Egyptians and Babylonians. It's just that some nations paid more attention to their angel than others, or had to call in prophets like Moses or Daniel to fathom their warnings. Israel's guardian is the archangel Michael.

The Jewish cabala also talks of 'preceptor' angels attached to the patriarchs. Thus Adam was watched over by the angel Raziel; Noah by Zaphkiel; Abraham by Zadkiel; Isaac and Tobias by Raphael; Joseph, Joshua and Daniel by Gabriel; Moses by Metatron and Solomon by Michael.

Nowhere in the Old Testament does it specifically say that all humans have guardian angels but there are hints, such as the popular Psalm 91 which goes: 'For he shall give his angels charge over thee, to keep thee in all thy ways. They shall bear thee up in their hands, lest thou dash thy foot against a stone.'

And when Abraham sent a servant to find a wife for his son Isaac, he declared that God would send Isaac's angel on ahead to arrange it all in advance, which apparently happened. (Genesis 24.7)

The apocryphal *The Book of Jubilees* (second century BC) seems to believe very definitely in guardian angels, though. Chapter 35 gives an expanded account of the famous sibling rivalry between Esau and Jacob (which incidentally explains better than the Bible why their father Isaac went along with the trick of the 'mess of pottage'. He simply thought the younger brother better suited to running the family business). At one point, to calm his wife's fears for Jacob, he says: 'And fear thou not on account of Jacob; for the guardian of Jacob is great and powerful and honoured, and praised more than the guardian of Esau.'

Whatever the exact belief earlier on, by Jesus' time it was commonly held by the Jews that everyone had their own guardian angel. Some sects, such as the Sadducees, denied it, but they were the minority. So when Peter was released from Herod's prison by 'an angel of the Lord' and went to his friends, they just could not believe Peter himself had escaped and assumed it must be his guardian angel, or spiritual double (Acts 12.15).

The aim of guardian angels is to channel as much light as possible from their world into ours. They are our mediators with higher powers. That is the purpose of the angelic hierarchy, according to Dionysius, to filter the ineffable wisdom and energy from the Fountain of Light at the heart of creation through progressively material levels till finally it reaches us in a form we can comprehend. Or, as he explains in Chapter 10:

All angels bring revelations and tidings of their superiors. The first bring word of the Godhead who is their inspiration, while the others, according to their rank, tell of those thus inspired by God... Furthermore, the prophets tell us that the holiest of the Seraphim "cry out to one another" [Isaiah 6.3] and it seems to me this shows that the first rank passes on to the second what they know of God... It is in accordance with this arrangement that each intelligent entity – as far as he properly can and to the extent he may – participates in that purification beyond purity – that superabundant Light, that perfection preceding all perfection. Nothing is perfect of itself. Nothing is completely free of the need for perfection. Nothing, that is, except that Being truly perfect in itself and truly preceding all perfection.

On the heavenly plane, guardian angels are most like us and their world overlaps our own, but they still have a very different perspective. From their sphere they can see all the patterns of events we are blind to. They try to help by sharing that insight with us but there seem quite definite limits to how far they can go. Much depends on how sensitive we are to their message.

Rarely outside war or personal crisis have people ever seen angels, however strongly they might feel or believe in their presence. If you piled up the instances they would make quite a mountain, but as a proportion of human experience it is tiny. Angels are mostly invisible. They also rarely intervene in any physical way. Miracles happen from time to time, but angelic guidance usually comes as nothing more concrete than an inspiration, the angel's whisper; or even just a spontaneous feeling of hope that leads the way out of a morass.

That is the natural way and perhaps it is just as well. Guardian angels are naturally comforting and share much of our view of the world, but even visions of them have sometimes alarmed the recipients. While visions of the higher angels, as in Ezekiel or Revelation, have often been terrifying.

ANGELS IN ART

Few people have actually seen angels. Most have depended on artists to give them a form for their mind's eye. As with playful little cherubs, Medieval artists after the

Nicene Council looked to classical pagan art for inspiration and quickly latched on to the images of winged Victories and others, such as Sleep and Death. This was not as strange as it may seem because many other Christian ideas were lifted straight from the ancient Greeks. It was decided that although they were by definition non-Christian, they had done wonders in the absence of divine revelation and were dubbed proto-Christians and given honorary places in heaven.

In the Bible, angels only have wings in blazing visions such as those of Ezekiel and Isaiah. When visiting earth on other divine business they simply adopted the form of 'men', and it often took a while for their hosts to realize they had special company. So in the earliest Christian art angels were simply portrayed as human. Then, thanks to classical art, they quickly acquired wings and haloes (to convey the impression of their shining countenances) and this basic form fitted people's idea of angels so well that it has remained ever since.

Medieval artists soon developed codes for wings and haloes. Seraphim were given red wings and cherubim blue ones. Haloes became circular, square or triangular according to who they were attached to. Triangular haloes, or three-pointed stars, denoted God or Jesus. Square haloes were for mortal saints (because a square was the symbol for earth). Angels had circular haloes to indicate they were direct offshoots from the divine whole. As the Middle Ages wore on, however, circular haloes became the norm for all divine beings.

Angels' wings are a triumph of beauty over science. Cynics from the Renaissance onwards have pointed out that angels would need breast bones like pigeons to fly, and the wings themselves would need a span of about forty feet. But this is missing the point entirely, which is that angels are not physical beings. They can adopt any form they like and choose whatever makes most sense to whoever they are visiting.

Winged angels look right even though our brains know they are biologically impossible. Astral travellers have even pointed out that the angels they meet in their visionary adventures do

in fact appear to have wings because their auras, radiating from the crown of the head and out beyond their astral bodies, give them that initial appearance. So possibly there was more than just classical influence at work. Possibly it was a case of visionary experience attaching itself to the closest existing models but, on the other hand, some people in dreams and trances still meet angels with no wings at all.

THE SEVEN HEAVENS

According to *The Book of Enoch* there are seven heavens and most people have accepted this. The nine choirs of angels are distributed between them more or less according to their rank in the hierarchy, though some seem to exist in several heavens at once, possibly because on one level they are in charge, while on another they are among equals.

The heavens are arranged in concentric spheres rather like Chinese puzzle-balls, only made of increasingly pure divine light. They also have the peculiar property that when you pass from an outer to an inner sphere it is by way of a point or gateway at the centre. When you pass through that you find yourself in another vast space, seemingly larger than the one you just left.

At the centre of each heaven is some echo of the Fountain of Light at the centre of the universe, usually taking the form of a blazing throne around which stand the angelic princes of that particular sphere.

The first heaven is said to be the paradise inhabited by Adam and Eve at the beginning of time. Here grow the Trees of Life and Knowledge and there is no death or sorrow to be found. Here dwell the guardian angels and the souls of those who have died but are watching over the friends and family they left behind. This is the garden that once could be found at the springs of the Tigris and Euphrates, till it was removed to a distance. In Hebrew it is called Shamayim and is ruled by the archangel Gabriel.

Here's what Enoch found there:

*A cloud then snatched me up, and the wind raised me above the surface of the earth, placing me at the extremity of the heavens. There I saw another vision; I saw the habitations and couches of the saints. There my eyes beheld their habitations with the angels, and their couches with the holy ones.
They were entreating, supplicating and praying for the sons of men; while righteousness like water flowed before them, and mercy like dew was scattered over the earth. And thus shall it be with them for ever and ever.*

THE BOOK OF ENOCH, CHAPTER 39 (RICHARD LAURENCE TRANSLATION, OXFORD UNIVERSITY PRESS, 1892)

There I beheld the fathers of the first men, and the saints who dwell in that place forever... I beheld the sons of the holy angels treading on flaming fire, whose garments and robes were white, and whose countenances were transparent as crystal... There I beheld, in the midst of that light, a building raised with stones of ice. And in the midst of these stones tongues of living fire, which encompassed it. Then the Seraphim, the Cherubim and Ophanim surrounded it; these are those who never sleep but watch the throne of his glory. And I beheld angels innumerable, thousands of thousands and myriads of myriads, who surrounded that habitation.

THE BOOK OF ENOCH, CHAPTER 70

Besides Dionysius, the prophet Enoch (or whoever assumed his name) is our greatest source of angel lore. According to Genesis, he was the seventh in line from Adam and the great-grandfather of Noah.

Enoch is also one of the few humans in the Bible said to have gone straight to heaven at the end without having to die. Genesis (Chapter 5.24) merely says enigmatically that after 365 years 'Enoch walked with God: and he was not; for God took him.' But esoteric tradition claims that not only did he go straight to heaven but he became (or possibly returned to being) the enigmatic archangel Metatron, of whom we have more later. He also made many earlier visionary visits to heaven which were the basis of his famous book.

The second heaven, Raquia (firmament) is ruled by the archangel Raphael. Enoch, Moses and St Paul are all said to have visited it, and it is where John the Baptist was supposed to have gone after death. As the name suggests, it was once believed to exist at the height of the firmament that 'divided the upper waters from those below' and in which the stars were fixed. The corresponding level in hell (which Enoch describes as adjoining the heaven 'in the north') is where most fallen angels dwell.

The third heaven is Sagun or Shehaqim ruled by the angel Anahel. St Paul was greeted here by an ancient man whose face shone like the sun, standing at a gate with pillars of gold. These are the famous 'pearly gates' because the third heaven is where perfect souls go straight after death. Like the first heaven, it has been described as having a garden or orchard where the Tree of Life grows. Many features seem to be shared by all the heavens, but they become more spiritually refined and further from our understanding on each level. Among the Essenes the Tree of Life was often shown with seven main branches reaching up to the seven heavens, and seven roots going down to the seven hells. This is very similar to the Teutonic concept of the Tree of Life.

The archangel Michael rules the fourth heaven, Zebhul. The fifth, Machon, is home to the Avenging Angels, stern dispensers of divine nemesis who are described at some length in the book of Job. It also holds large numbers of the more friendly Virtues who

In solitude she lived,
And in solitude built her lonely nest;
And in solitude, alone
Hath the Beloved guided her,
In solitude also wounded with love.
St John of the Cross

Bound up with love in one eternal book, the scattered leaves of all the universe.
DANTE: *THE DIVINE COMEDY*

govern the courses of the stars and planets and the unfolding of human destiny. In fact, despite the general biblical disapproval of astrology, these Virtues seem to correspond exactly with the planetary gods used in horoscopes.

The sixth and seventh heavens are so far beyond our understanding that all that can be said with certainty is that they are home to vast choirs of angels chanting the Song of Creation. At the very centre stand the cherubim and seraphim and finally the unknowable Godhead itself, or Fountain of Light. Or possibly, of course, it might just be the portal to another series of heavens.

In shadowy reflection of these seven heavens are seven hells with corresponding legions of devils and demons. Enoch describes them all adjoining the heavens 'in the north', though given the tricky nature of heavenly geography this is probably more symbolic than anything. According to Enoch, it means that in heaven there is a running war along the frontier. Angels and demons not only fight through us in our world – their main arena – but face to face on the frontiers of heaven.

The symmetry of all this suggests we must all be born with a guardian demon as well as an angel. This gets much less talked about, but in a way it is implicit in the old idea of having a light and dark angel on each shoulder.

To many people the terms 'guardian angel' and 'spirit guide' are interchangeable but there is an important distinction that is perhaps worth mentioning here. Spirit guides are generally humans who have died, while angels are, of course, immortal. They are more like the 'higher self' that many people feel directing their lives. Among Indian mystics it is commonly accepted that one's guru can be a wholly spiritual being or deva.

Some mystics have also claimed that we are simply the incarnation of our guardian angel or higher self, that after death we wake to this realization for a while, before choosing to be born again in circumstances that will aid our evolution as angels. As we saw with Enoch and Metatron, there are hints of this in ancient Jewish belief and even in the whole story of Christ's incarnation. The possibility also bridges the gap between the biblical religions and others that preach reincarnation, but it has never been accepted in mainstream Christianity, Judaism or Islam. For some reason they have always been hostile to the idea of earthly reincarnation being common, unlike most other faiths. Jesus and a few prophets were seen as the great exceptions.

CHAPTER THREE

Angels of the Nativity

And there in the same country shepherds abiding in the
field, keeping watch over their flock by night.
And lo, the angel of the Lord came upon them.

LUKE 2

ngels are inseparable from the story of Jesus, especially at its starry beginning. The tale of the nativity is shared between the Gospels and it is Luke (Chaper 1) who begins with the tale of Jesus' forerunner, John the Baptist. We hear how the angel Gabriel, 'that stands in the presence of God', appeared to his father in the temple to tell of the birth, and how Zacharias was struck temporarily dumb because he found it hard to believe, seeing how old he and his wife were. Then we hear of Gabriel's famous vision to the Virgin Mary bringing similar news. Matthew (Chapter 1) takes up the story with how the angel appeared to Joseph in a dream to calm his fears, then back to Luke (Chapter 2) for half the magical account of the Nativity that still moves us today:

And the angel said unto them: 'Fear not: for, behold, I bring you good tidings of great joy, which shall be to all people. For unto you is born this day in the city of David a Saviour, which is Christ the Lord. And this shall be a sign unto you; Ye shall find the babe wrapped in swaddling clothes, lying in a manger.' And suddenly there was with the angel a multitude of the heavenly host praising God, and singing: 'Glory to God in the highest, and on earth peace and good will towards men.'

And it came to pass, as the angels were gone away from them into heaven, the shepherds said one to another: 'Let us now go even unto Bethlehem, and see this thing which is come to pass, which the Lord hath made known unto us.'

And they came with haste, and found Mary, and Joseph, and the babe lying in a manger. And when they had seen it, they made known abroad the saying which was told them concerning this child. And all they that heard it wondered at those things which were told them by the shepherds. But Mary kept all these things, and pondered them in her heart. And the shepherds returned, glorifying and praising God for all the things that they had heard and seen, as it was told unto them.

GABRIEL

The angel Gabriel, who is so prominent in the Nativity tale, is one of the few in the Bible with a name. Gabriel is also unusual for having strong female overtones and has often even been painted as a female.

Other female angels crept into angelic choirs in the background of art in the Middle Ages, but in subordinate roles. The archangels are almost invariably considered and shown as male, apart from Gabriel and, very occasionally, Raphael. Even while not obviously female, Gabriel is often shown holding a lily, a coded sign of femininity. Perhaps this was because of the association with fertility and birth. In any other culture Gabriel would have been a goddess.

As in other areas, art was often ahead of the theologians in humane terms, in softening the message. In theology the idea of Gabriel being female came close to heresy and angels are all called 'he' in the Bible, if not completely lacking in gender (Matthew 22.30: 'For in the resurrection they neither marry nor are given in marriage, but are like the angels in heaven.' (See also Mark 12.25.)

Swedenbourg contradicted this by claiming that angels, since they derived from humans, are both male and female and even engage in spiritual marriage. But this was another idea of his that failed to catch on.

The problem in Judaic mythology is that the feminine aspect of God, the Shekinah, was so firmly banished to the esoteric fringes, along with Adam's demonized first wife Lilith, that it almost obliged angels to be male.

In Gnostic Christianity the Shekinah was identified with Sophia or Wisdom to whom many psalms are dedicated. Sophia was both mother and lover of the major archons (roughly equivalent to archangels in both camps). After a while however she grew tired of her heavenly lovers and became curious about the physical world below. When she left them to explore it, the archons' jealousy trapped her there and forced her into prostitution. After many ages of this humiliation Sophia escaped through her patient application of wisdom.

She was restored to the highest sphere of heaven where, in one apocryphal text, she says: 'I am the first and last, the honoured and despised, the whore and the holy one, wife and virgin, barren and fecund.'

In the Gnostic cult devoted to her, Mary Magdalene was seen as having re-enacted Sophia's drama in her own life. As with the prodigal son, what made her virtue so special was that it had been acquired through experience, suffering and finally insight, instead of blind obedience.

However, all this fascinating metaphysical drama was deemed heretical by the early Church and had to surface in other ways, such as the legends that stubbornly clung to Magdalene and which built up around the Virgin Mary and the supposedly male angel Gabriel.

In comparative mythology, Gabriel has often been equated with Astarte or Ishtar and it has often been recommended that expectant mothers call upon Gabriel to see them safely through labour. One legend says it is Gabriel who chooses the souls that are to be born and instructs them during their nine months in the womb, finally silencing them and casting a spell of forgetfulness by pressing a finger to their lips. This, it is said, is the cause of the sharp indent on the upper lip so characteristic of newborn babies.

Gabriel is also the angel of the Moon, the most female of the major luminaries. In New Age circles he has often been renamed 'Gabrielle' but Gabriel in the Bible was also responsible for many resolutely 'masculine' deeds. Possibly what has happened is that two totally different entities have ended up with the same name. This is quite likely because only three angelic names made it into the canon of the Bible, so all appearances tended to be attributed to one or other of them.

MUSIC OF THE SPHERES

The Nativity shepherds are far from being the only people to have heard choirs of angels in full song. Heavenly symphonies and vast choruses usually do accompany their appearance, as countless witnesses have testified from ancient times to the present.

Angels and music are inseparable. When not chanting the Music of Creation in vast choirs, circling like swans around the Fountain of Light at the heart of creation, measuring the unfolding of the universe in endlessly complex but effortless harmonies, angels in art and legend can be found playing every musical instrument imaginable. Music is their primary language, as Dante describes it:

> *Motion matched with motion, song with song –*
> *Song that surpassed in sweetness and delight*
> *The singing of our Muses or our sirens,*
> *Even as a ray surpasses its reflection.*
>
> DANTE, *THE DIVINE COMEDY*: 'PARADISO', CANTO 12

Angels are also said to have a form of speech and script of their own that is unintelligible to humans. Many ingenious forgeries are in circulation – whole books in fact, which might well contain the secrets of the universe if anyone could unravel the characters. The most famous is that supposedly written by the archangel Raziel and given by him to Adam after his expulsion from Eden. It was said to contain 'all celestial and earthly knowledge' no less. A key section in the middle of the book is said to contain in secret writing the 1500 keys to the mystery of the world that not even angels possessed.

From Adam this book passed to Enoch (who has been accused of having borrowed much from it for his own book) then Noah and Solomon, who learned most of his wisdom from it. Some believe it has survived to this day as the elusive *Sefer Raziel* or *Book of the Angel Raziel*. There are even antiquarian copies in circulation, but they are assumed to be Medieval forgeries.

Gregorian chant, Bach, Beethoven and Handel all conjure visions of angelic orchestras and choirs, but composers who have actually been inspired by celestial music complain about how far short they fall in recapturing it. The best they can do is catch a flavour or a few strands of the original which then have to be reworked in the composer's idiom. This is despite the apparent attempts of some angelic visitors to adapt their music to the capacity of their audience, even down to the musical instruments they choose.

There are countless examples of musicians and others being inspired by angels, but just a few of the more famous ones will serve our purpose. The great instigator of the tradition was St John, author of the book of Revelation, who apparently managed to recall some of the angelic hymns from his famous vision on the Isle of Patmos. For a while they were famous but have been lost or corrupted through the ages. The Venerable Bede (c.675–735 AD), clear-headed historian of the early Anglo Saxons in Britain, has an interesting tale to tell about the earliest known English hymn-writer, Caedmon, who died about 680 AD.

Caedmon composed a vast number of hymns in the early English language that played a vital part in converting the Anglo Saxons to Christianity. Before him there was no easy way of conveying the Christian message because the scriptures were in Latin, and even then copies were very rare and hardly anyone could read. Song and verse were the main cultural media and the early Saxon Church had nothing to match the vigorous pagan heritage of those it was trying to convert.

Caedmon himself seemed to lack any musical talent till late in life. He was a labourer on the estates of Whitby Abbey and was so unmusical that when, as was the custom, the harp was passed round after dinner, he used to slip off to the stables rather than embarrass himself. On one such occasion he went off to tend the beasts and fell asleep in the hay.

In his dreams a 'man' suddenly appeared and said: 'Caedmon, sing me something.'

'I don't know how to sing,' Caedmon replied. 'That's why I left the feast.'

The stranger said: 'But you shall sing for me.'

'What should I sing about?' asked Caedmon.

'Sing about the creation of the world,' replied the stranger.

And in his dream Caedmon found himself singing a perfectly wonderful hymn he had never heard before in his life. It began something like this, though much of the magic has been lost through copying and translation:

> Praise we now the weaver of Heaven's fabric,
> The majesty of his might and mind's wisdom,
> Work of the world-warden, worker of all wonders.
> How he the Lord of glory everlasting
> Wrought first for men Heaven as a roof-tree,
> Then made Middle Earth to be their mansion.

The next morning Caedmon could remember not only his dream but every detail of the hymn he had sung. He rushed into the abbey and was taken before the abbess, to whom he told his tale and sang the hymn again. Everyone was enchanted and agreed that an angel of God must indeed have blessed Caedmon. They asked if he could try making another hymn on a different theme, and the following morning he returned with a new song just as beautiful.

Beyond the hills a watered land,
Beyond the gulf a gleaming strand
Of mansions where the righteous sup;
Who sleep at ease among their trees,
Or wake to sing a cadenced hymn
With Cherubim and Seraphim.
CHRISTINA ROSSETTI, *THE CONVENT THRESHOLD*

After this he was persuaded to become a monk and began the regular practice of dictating a hymn each morning to some monks, being completely illiterate himself. Then he would sit down and become their pupil in the scriptures for the rest of the day. In effect, he became the Bible's translator into simple, tuneful Anglo-Saxon verse, which was far more potent than any preaching because it came straight from his heart and soul.

As Bede tells it: 'He sang of the creation of the world, the origin of the human race and the whole story of Genesis. He sang of Israel's exodus from Egypt, the entry into the Promised Land, and many other events of scriptural history. He sang of the Lord's Incarnation, Passion, Resurrection and Ascension into heaven, the coming of the Holy Spirit and the teaching of the Apostles.' He also composed many other hymns of his own volition, 'And so crowned his life with a happy end.'

Sadly all but the above fragment from Bede has been lost, but Caedmon's songs had vast influence at the time, and although many others tried his composing method, none succeeded nearly as well.

Leaping forward in time, Joseph Haydn (1732–1809) was also dependent on angelic favour for his work, though less so than Caedmon. When he hit a block in composing his great oratorio, *The Creation*, rather than racking his brains for inspiration he searched his soul for imperfections that might be blocking its flow. He also claimed no credit for his wonderful chorus 'Let there be Light', which he composed near the end of his life, but claimed: 'It all came to me from above.'

Handel, too, on finishing writing his famous 'Hallelujah Chorus', was found in tears by his servant and declared that for a time 'I did think I did see all Heaven before me, and the great God Himself.' Handel's *Messiah* was composed in a mere 24 days, during which he hardly ate and later said: 'Whether I was in the body or out of my body when I wrote it I know not.'

Appropriately enough, angels are said to have inspired many Christmas carols, such as the tune for 'O Little Town of Bethlehem'. The words were by Phillips Brooks, rector in the 1860s of Trinity Church in Boston, one of America's greatest preachers and, later, Bishop of Massachussets. Having written the verses, he asked his organist Lewis Redner to come up with a tune. The poor man was stumped till Christmas Eve, when he dreamed of angels singing a melody that he wrote down upon waking. The hymn, which we still sing today, was, according to Redner, a gift from angels.

Another famous pastor, William Cushing, discovered a musical talent in 1876 after losing his ability to speak. While praying for guidance for his future, since he was unable to preach, he received a vision of paradise. It was accompanied by a hymn he managed to write down, thus beginning a new vocation as many of his hymns were soon being sung around the world. He is perhaps best known now for 'Jewels (When He Comes)'.

Many people who recall visions of angels and heavenly light during near-death experiences also mention music. It is part of the sense of bliss and liberation that makes them reluctant to return to their lives when it is explained that they are not yet ready to shuffle off their mortal coil. It is interesting that such visions seem to happen as often to atheists and agnostics as to believers, which suggests that angels are far less concerned by people's religious affiliations than with the kind of person they are.

In Islam, the patron angel of music is Israfel ('the Fiery One') who is destined to blow the trumpet on Judgement Day. Israfel is said to have accompanied Mohammed for three years to prepare him for his great work, after which time Gabriel took over. Another Islamic legend says that at the Creation God sent Israfel, Michael, Gabriel and Azrael to the four corners of the earth to fetch dust for the making of Adam. However, Israfel is not actually mentioned by name in the Koran.

CHAPTER FOUR

DIVINE MESSENGERS

*And there appeared unto him an angel of the Lord
standing on the right side of the altar of incense.*

LUKE 1

The word angel comes from the Roman *angelus* or Greek *aggelos* meaning simply 'messenger'. In Persian and Sanskrit it is *angaros*, while in Hebrew angels are called *mall'akh*, which also means 'messenger', because the main purpose of angels in the Bible is simply to bear messages from God to His people. Some do intervene directly, for instance in leading the Israelites out of Egypt, destroying the armies of Sennacherib when they besieged Jerusalem, or rescuing the apostles from prison. Their usual purpose, though, is simply to convey God's intentions or warnings.

God Himself rarely makes a direct appearance. Occasionally, He seems to address

His prophets directly, or appear in their visions as the Ancient of Days or the Burning Bush. More often, He sends an angel to do the work. So much so that John asserts confidently at the beginning of his Gospel that: 'No man has seen God at any time' (John 1.18).

Angels are a concept particularly native to the Middle East. In other cultures gods and goddesses (or faeries among the ancient Celts) played the same role. But once the idea of a single supreme deity took shape it became necessary to create another class for the beings who operated on the divine level but were not actually gods (in Genesis even the Bible refers to them as that).

Angels were not just a Jewish concept, as the Jews borrowed ideas freely from their neighbours, particularly the Babylonians among whom they lived during the Exile. Many angels are in fact simply Babylonian deities in disguise, something freely acknowledged in the Jewish Talmud *Rosch Haschanna 56*, which mentions that the angels' names were introduced from Babylon.

The fire-worshipping Zoroastrians of Persia also had an enormous influence on Jewish and Christian belief that is now largely forgotten. Many of Enoch's visions, which shaped those of early Christianity, are almost identical to Zoroastrian views of the spiritual world. These were revealed to the prophet Zoroaster (or Zarathustra) by an angel called Vohu Manah (Good Mind) in about 500 BC, just as the Koran was dictated to Mohammed a millennium or so later by the angel Gabriel. Even the concept of the seven angels who 'stand before God' is Zoroastrian and angels are intimately associated with fire.

Angels are mediators between humans and an entity too dazzling for us to face directly without being utterly consumed. Even Enoch, during his visits to heaven, had to be 'veiled' to avoid being destroyed by what he saw.

There are angels corresponding to every level of Paradise, from the first, which is very like an idealized or purified Earth, to those beyond comprehension and which visionaries such as William Blake could only describe in terms of glowing rings of ever more purified, singing light. Some angels are with us constantly, guardian angels and the principalities that watch over nations and cities and all collective human enterprises.

Others are more remote. Their natural homes are the inner spheres of heaven and (apart from a few archangels who seem at home on every level) they only occasionally and in dire circumstances venture out into our world. They are the ones most privy to the Divine Will and ignoring their message is always disastrous.

Besides guardian angels, archangels are the ones most familiar to us. Most of us can name at least three: Michael, Gabriel and Raphael, who are the only three mentioned by name in the Bible (though Raphael is only to be found in the Catholic Bible that includes *The Book of Tobit*). September 29 is celebrated as a Catholic feast for these three, who are widely accepted as being the three angels who visited Abraham (Genesis 18).

Archangels are strange in that they rank only second in the celestial hierarchy, yet their chiefs are also the rulers of the seraphim and cherubim, the highest ranks. They seem to exist on many levels simultaneously. Michael and Gabriel for instance are seraphim and so closest to the divine Source. But in the Bible, they are also God's most active messengers to our world. They are at the same time closest to the Fountain of Light and second closest to our world, with which they are intimately concerned, because this is supposed to be the main battleground in the ongoing war between heaven and hell.

It's not always clear if there are four or seven archangels, or if these are just the leaders of countless others. But almost everyone agrees that the four main archangels are Michael, Gabriel, Raphael and Uriel (or Phanuel). Most others accept that there were seven 'angels of the Presence', of whom these were the main four. There is almost no agreement with regard to the other three.

Enoch names them as Raguel, Seraqeal and Haniel. Pseudo-Dionysius lists them as Chamuel, Jophiel and Zadkiel. Zadkiel is commonly mentioned elsewhere but the only other broad agreement is that the archangels included Satan or Lucifer before his fall.

ARCHANGELS

Michael

This name means 'Who is as God', because throughout Christianity, Islam and Judaism Michael is accepted as the greatest of all the angels, the one closest to God since Satan's rebellion. Michael led the heavenly hosts against the rebel angels and is destined to do so again in the great battle at the end of time. In the Dead Sea scroll 'The War of the Sons of Light against the Sons of Darkness', which gives an account of the famous battle so conspicuously missing from the Bible, Michael leads the heavenly hosts against Belial, the Prince of Darkness, or Satan.

Michael is the leader of the seraphim, principalities and other ranks besides archangels. Enoch says he 'presides over human virtue and commands the nations', particularly the nation of Israel of which he is the guardian. The Chaldeans worshipped the archangel Michael as a god and he has also been equated with Saosyhant the Redeemer in the Avesta, the Zoroastrian holy book.

And there was war in heaven: Michael and his angels fought against the dragon; and the dragon fought and his angels, and prevailed not; neither was their place found any more in heaven.
REVELATION 12

Michael is often named as the angel who appeared to Moses in the burning bush (Exodus 3.2). Legend says he also fought with Satan for Moses' body after he died. He was also the angel sent to Daniel when he was suffering at Nebuchadnezzar's hands (Daniel 3.28: 6.22), though some say it was Gabriel. In Jewish mysticism Michael is called the 'glory' of the Shekinah, the female aspect of God who became estranged from Him when Adam and Eve were expelled from paradise. Some say the whole purpose of the Torah, or Jewish faith, is to reunite the male and female aspects of the Divinity.

The cherubim were formed from the tears Michael shed over human sins, though on other occasions his tears merely turned into precious stones. As well as being God's principal messenger to us, he is the chief pleader with God for mercy on our behalf. Jewish tradition names him as the author of Psalm 85, which praises God for turning aside from anger towards His people.

Michael is usually portrayed with sword and armour, showing that he is the battle-

leader of the heavenly hosts. He also often holds a pair of scales because, as dispenser of Divine justice, it is he who will weigh souls on the Day of Judgement. In this he is related to the Egyptian Anubis and both have been identified with the star Sirius.

Michael is most often shown fighting a dragon (i.e. Satan) though in art the human St George gradually replaced him. In comparative mythology Michael is equated with Mercury or the Greek Hermes, conductor of souls to the land of the dead and patron of all forms of communication, especially music. So it was Michael who told the Virgin Mary of her impending death, just as Gabriel announced her Immaculate Conception. There are also several other angels of death, each responsible for particular groups such as children, warriors and kings.

Churches dedicated to St Michael in Europe were often built over temples dedicated to Mercury or Hermes, or in places associated with dragons, such as St Michael's Mount in both Cornwall and Brittany, which, from prehistoric times, were associated with Earth Powers.

In astrology Michael is equated with the sun, planetary ruler of the star sign Leo.

Gabriel

As we saw earlier, Gabriel ('God is my strength'), has many female connotations but is determinedly male in, for example, the book of Daniel. There he appears in Chapter 8 to explain Daniel's vision concerning Alexander the Great's conquest of the Persian Empire, and again in Chapter 9 concerning another vision. Gabriel is also said to be the angel who poured destruction on Sodom and Gomorrah.

Elsewhere though, particularly in Enoch, Gabriel sits on the left side of God in the seventh heaven. This place is where one might expect to find God's wife and again suggests that, if not actually female, Gabriel constitutes a feminine force.

Gabriel is simultaneously ruler of the cherubim in the seventh heaven and a ruler of the guardian angels in the first, where most

mortals go after death. S/he is also the preceptor of Jesus' foster father Joseph and is said to be the angel who inspired Joan of Arc.

In Babylonian legend, Gabriel was banished from the Presence for a time for failing to carry out God's commands exactly. Dobiel, Persia's guardian angel, stood in for a while till peace was restored.

In Islamic tradition, Gabriel (or Jibril of the 140 pairs of wings) is the Angel of Truth who dictated the Koran to Mohammed, verse by verse. Also in Islamic tradition there is some confusion between Gabriel and the Holy Ghost, which again hints at the feminine, because even in Christianity there have been speculations that the Holy Ghost represents God's feminine aspect. Gabriel is also one of the angels who comforted Jesus in Gethsemane on the eve of the Crucifixion.

In astrology, Gabriel is equated with the moon, planetary ruler of the sign Cancer.

Raphael

Raphael ('Healer of God') belongs to several orders of angels (seraphim, cherubim, dominions and powers) but his particular duties are to rule the guardian angels in the first heaven and to inspire healers in both the physical and psychic fields. Raphael is said to be the most friendly and approachable of the archangels and even to have a sense of humour, which is rare among the higher angels!

In *The Book of Tobit* (which can be found in the Catholic Bible) he teaches Tobit's scatterbrained son Tobias the medicinal value of parts of a certain fish they catch, and how some could be used to exorcize demons. This soon came in very handy because Tobias became engaged to marry someone whose seven previous fiancés had been killed on their wedding night (before they could enjoy her favours) by the jealous demon Asmodeus, who had fallen in love with her.

As a healer, Raphael helped soothe the pain of Abraham's circumcision late in life, and healed Jacob's thigh when he dislocated it wrestling another angel (Genesis 32), who has been variously named as all the chief archangels and even God himself. Raphael is also the patron of other sciences. He advised Noah on building his Ark and helped Solomon with his temple.

Raphael was originally a Chaldean deity named Labbiel and, in *The Book of Tobit*, declares that he is one of the seven holy angels who stand before the throne of God (Tobit 12.15). He is also one of the seven angels of the Apocalypse and is often named Regent of the Sun, though this title is more often assigned to Uriel. Raphael is the ruling Prince of the second heaven and chief guardian of the Tree of Life. He was the preceptor angel of Isaac.

In astrology Raphael is equated with Mercury, planetary ruler of the star signs Gemini and Virgo.

Uriel

Uriel ('Flame of God') is described in *The Book of Enoch* as being the angel who 'presides over clamour and terror'. That is to say, like Michael he is one of the angelic war-leaders against the rebel angels. In the book of Revelation it is probably Uriel who, as Regent of the Sun, summons the birds of the air to feast upon the fallen. He is also ruler of Tartarus, the land of the dead. Some say it was Uriel who warned Noah of the coming Flood, although in *The Book of Enoch* it is Enoch himself who does this, as much of the book is addressed to Noah.

In the year 745 AD, a church council under Pope Zachary decided that everyone was taking far too much interest in angels and demoted Uriel and all other angels not actually named in the Bible. Thereafter earthly saints were promoted as the patrons of various human activities and gradually took over the duties of angels. On the surface this was quite successful and for most Christians angels gradually became shadowy,

And he dreamed, and behold a ladder set up on the earth, and the top of it reached to heaven.

GENESIS 28

nameless hosts largely confined to heaven. But on the mystical fringes of Christianity, angel lore continued to flourish.

Despite his demotion, Uriel remained very popular and appears in Milton's *Paradise Lost*, gliding through the evening on a sunbeam. He is also one of the main candidates for being the angel who wrestled with Jacob at Peniel (Genesis 32) as a result of which Jacob's name was changed to Israel and he became leader of his people. Other candidates include Michael, Metatron and even God Himself. But Uriel is most likely because one of his other names is often given as Jacob-Israel, hinting at some swapping or sharing of personalities that may have taken place at the wrestling match.

It has been suggested that Jacob was in fact an incarnation of his 'preceptor' angel Uriel, and the fight was because he was refusing to accept this, and the challenges it entailed.

According to the most common Jewish tradition, it was Uriel who smote the Assyrian King Sennacherib's host as it besieged Jerusalem 'with a sharpened scythe which had been ready since Creation'. He killed 185,000 of his troops in one night with the result that, when Sennacherib went home in disgrace, he was murdered by his own sons (2 Kings 18–19; Isaiah 36–37).

Phanuel and Chamuel seem to be other names for the same angel.

In astrology Uriel is equated with Mars, planetary ruler of the signs Aries and Scorpio.

Anael

Anael is one of the seven angels of the Creation and chief of the principalities. His particular concern is with human sexuality and, as a ruler of the second heaven, with watching over traffic between it and the first. Anael is often confused or identified with Ariel, whose name Shakespeare borrowed for his sprite in *The Tempest*. Ariel ('Lion of God') is often depicted with a lion's head and is said to be the guardian angel of Jerusalem. Confusingly, Ariel is also frequently described as one of the fallen angels in charge of punishments in the underworld. Possibly there were two angels with the same name. Good and evil angels are often twinned in this way, with suggestions that they may even be one and the same being merely acting out different roles in heaven and hell. But this leads to some very tricky questions about morality and the nature of evil that no one has yet managed to resolve.

In astrology Anael is equated with Venus, planetary ruler of the signs Taurus and Libra.

Zadkiel

Zadkiel (meaning 'Righteousness of God') is often portrayed holding a dagger, because it is widely believed he was the angel who kept Abraham from sacrificing his son Isaac in the famous test of loyalty. With Jophiel, he is one of the two standard bearers who immediately follow Michael into battle. Zadkiel is also called the angel of benevolence, mercy and memory, is leader of the angelic order of dominions and is one of the seven archangels who stand in the presence of God.

In astrology, Zadkiel is equated with Jupiter, planetary ruler of Pisces and Sagittarius.

O, not in cruelty, not in wrath
The Reaper came that day;
'Twas an angel visited the earth
And took the flowers away.
LONGFELLOW

Cassiel

Cassiel (meaning 'Speed of God') is almost nowhere mentioned as one of the seven angels closest to God, but he is supposed to be a ruling prince of the seventh heaven and is most often suggested as the angelic counterpart of Saturn.

Not much is actually known about Cassiel beyond him being described as 'the angel of solitudes and tears who shows forth the unity of the eternal kingdom'. He is the angel of temperance and patience, in keeping with the positive aspects of the zodiacal Saturn. Further, he is one of the chief angels of death who, like Saturn in his aspect of the Grim Reaper, comes to lead souls to heaven. Cassiel's particular concern is the death of kings and he is only grim to the extent that few people actually feel quite ready to see his face when their time comes. In the Jewish Zohar, Cassiel is Gabriel's chief standard bearer in battle, along with the angel Hizkiel. In astrology Cassiel (or Zaphkiel) is equated with Saturn, planetary ruler of Aquarius and Capricorn.

Metatron

The above are the seven angels corresponding to the planetary gods of astrology. Whether all seven are also the 'angels of the Presence' is debatable because many others have been suggested. The list is extensive, so only the most striking will be discussed.

One of the most mysterious of all angels is Metatron, whose very name is unusual, since it doesn't end in –el, as the others do. Metatron is often confused with Michael but seems to have a quite distinct identity. As with Michael, Metatron is often called the supreme angel, prince of the Divine Presence and even the Lesser Jehovah, which has suggested to many that beyond the archangels are other levels of beings who mediate with the Divine on the archangels' behalf.

In Jewish tradition, Metatron is often said to be superior to Michael and Gabriel and was able to eject Jannes and Jambre, two Egyptian wizards who infiltrated heaven by magic, when the other archangels failed. Some say Metatron was incarnated on earth for a while as the prophet Enoch who, when he returned to heaven, was restored to angelic form as a spirit of fire with 36 pairs of wings covered with countless eyes. When invoked in cabalistic rites, Metatron most commonly appears as a pillar of flame with a face more dazzling than the sun. He is believed to be the angel who guided the Israelites through the desert after their escape from Egypt in the form of a pillar of fire by night and smoke by day (Exodus 13.21).

Metatron is said to be the largest of the angels and lives in the seventh heaven right beside the Throne of God. He is the twin of the angel Sandalphon who has sometimes been called the female cherub on the Ark of the Covenant. As such, Metatron and Sandalphon are counterparts of Jehovah and Shekinah, the male and female aspects of Divinity. But Sandalphon, despite this femininity was apparently incarnated as the prophet Elijah who, like Enoch, ascended to heaven at the end of his life without having to die.

The origins of the name Metatron are obscure but opinion has it that it means 'he who occupies the throne next to God'.

Raziel

Raziel (meaning 'Secret of God') is another patron of learning, particularly of mystical lore, being the 'angel of the secret regions and chief of the Supreme Mysteries'. Raziel is the supposed author of the book we mentioned earlier containing all the mysteries of the world. Whether or not *The Book of the Angel Raziel* in circulation today is a forgery, it is a treasure house of angelic lore which is still worth plundering. Legend has it that other angels were jealous when he gave it to Adam. They threw the book into the ocean but God ordered Rahab, the angel of the deep, to fish it out and return it.

According to Jewish tradition the archangel Raziel stands on Mount Horeb each day and proclaims the secrets of men to the whole world. He is chief of the order of thrones or Erelim, the 'valiant ones' mentioned in Isaiah 33.7, who are said to be made of white fire and have special charge of grass, trees, fruit and grain.

Ramiel

Ramiel (meaning 'Mercy of God') stands beside Michael when souls are weighed and afterwards leads them to paradise (if they pass the test). He is also the bestower of true visions and is often equated with Uriel. In the apocryphal *Apocalypse of Baruch*, Ramiel is named as the angel who interprets Baruch's vision and appears to be the one who destroyed Sennacherib's hosts. Enoch names Ramiel as both an archangel and a fallen one, though perhaps two angels have the same name. In Milton's *Paradise Lost*, Ramiel features as a fallen angel who is defeated on the first day of the battle in heaven.

These are just the most famous archangels. They are the main candidates for being in the select group immediately surrounding God in the seventh heaven. Cabalism and other esoteric studies have proposed countless others, but often they are just different names for the same few beings. It seems possible, though, that the four or seven principal archangels are just the princes of a large order of archangels about whom little is known. It has also been suggested that all angels above the first rank may be termed 'archangels', which means they are countless in number.

The Koran mentions four archangels but names only Michael and Gabriel. Tradition names the other two Azrael (also known as Ariel) and Israfel, the angel of music.

CHAPTER FIVE

ANGELIC CHOIRS
THE HEAVENLY HIERARCHY

Thus, in the semblance of a snow-white rose,
There was displayed to me the saintly throng.
Just like a swarm of bees, which at one time
Alight upon the flowers, and then again
Return to where their savoury toil is stored.
Their countenances were of living flame,
Their wings of finest gold; the rest of them
Was whiter than the whiteness of snow.

DANTE, *THE DIVINE COMEDY:* 'PARADISO', CANTO 31

*B*ecause music is so essential to angels, their hierarchy is arranged into choirs. The choirs are also their regiments in time of angelic war. Their main duty, however, is singing and playing the music of the spheres and this is in some way an active thing. Their music helps the universe unfold, helping the Light filter from the centre to its outermost recesses. The way in which music sometimes lifts our souls is but the palest reflection of how angelic music operates.

There are arguments over details but most lists of angels agree broadly with that of Pseudo-Dionysius. Disagreements have focused mainly on the exact order of the middle choirs, the powers, principalities and virtues. On the identity of the first and last groups (seraphim, cherubim, archangels and angels) there is more or less complete agreement.

Pseudo-Dionysius divided angels into nine choirs, beginning with the seraphim and cherubim who inhabit the circles or spheres closest to God. There is some confusion between these two orders, and over which comes first, but as both are so far removed from our own reality this is not to be taken too seriously. Dionysius further divided the choirs into three triads and suggested that each order was likely to be further divided into triads.

Third Triad	*Second Triad*	*First Triad*
Angels	Powers	Thrones
Archangels	Virtues (Authorities)	Cherubim
Principalities	Dominions	Seraphim

*T*HIRD TRIAD

We have already looked at angels and archangels so, moving on up through the hierarchy, the next order we come to is that of the principalities.

Principalities

The principalities are angels who watch over large groups of humans and their rulers. So each town, city and nation is said to have its own principality, as do political and religious movements. As Michael was (or is) the principality of Israel, so Dobiel was the angel of Persia and Mastema the angel of Egypt. Pseudo-Dionysius explains those countries' occasional hostility to Israel as being due to their lack of attunement with their

own principality. This came from them not accepting one supreme God and so being blind to his purpose. It is occasionally clear that nations fall under the sway of some fallen angel intent on leading them to disaster. Or perhaps their principality goes over to Satan, as is said to have happened with Mastema.

The principalities also watch over the angels below them and are responsible for passing on to them divine inspiration from above. Their equivalents in Islamic lore are the djinns who are also usually tied to particular localities. In Jordan today, especially around the rock temple of Petra, one can still find shrines in the wilderness dedicated to angels of the locality that are maintained by passing travellers.

Princes of the principalities include Haniel (leader), Requel, Cerviel and Nisroch, who was their leader before his fall. Nisroch was originally an Assyrian deity worshipped by Sennacherib and is often portrayed as having a human form, but with wings and the head of an eagle.

$\mathcal{S}$ECOND TRIAD

Moving on, we come to the second triad of the angelic hierarchy consisting of powers, virtues and dominions.

Powers (Potentates)

The powers are widely believed to be the first order of angels to be created by God after the seven archangels, and are the most active in the constant war between heaven and hell. Dionysius says of them: 'They stop the efforts of demons who would overthrow the world.' Perhaps because of this frequent contact they are also the angels most liable to contamination and going over to the other side. Most of the fallen angels are said to come from the order of the powers.

The powers on either side of the divide are the angels most concerned with battling for control of our world and it was because of his difficulty in telling them apart that St Paul often warned against getting involved with them. Paul is largely responsible for the Church's hostility towards angels but ironically it is largely because he happened to mention so many kinds in passing (Ephesians 1.21; Colossians 1.16) that they could not be swept under the carpet. Having been named by Paul as real, his followers were obliged to keep taking angels into some sort of account.

The main duty of the powers is to keep the heavenly highways open so that all the other angels can communicate freely, and to prevent the infiltration of heaven by demons. In *Paradise Lost*, Milton describes them almost as border guards, a heavenly rapid response group forever on the alert for encroachment by the enemy. Spiritualists believe it is the powers who guide lost souls through the maze of the Astral Plane if they lose their way after death, particularly when they have died suddenly and without time to prepare themselves for the journey.

Their leader is the archangel Chamuel (or 'he who seeks God'). Chamuel is also leader of the choir of dominations and is often mentioned as one of the seven angels who 'stand before God'. Chamuel was one of Gabriel's companions in comforting Jesus in the Garden of Gethsemane before his ordeal. Like Michael he is a mediator between the Israelites and God, standing at the window of heaven to hear their prayers.

Chamuel appears to be the twin of Camael (or Kemuel), the Prince of Hell who tried to prevent Moses receiving the Torah on Mount Sinai. Camael also appears as a monstrous leopard in Revelation. The twins are often related to the warlike planet Mars, in both its positive and negative aspects.

Virtues (Authorities, Malakim or Tarshishim)

Also known as the 'Shining Ones', the virtues were midwives to Eve when giving birth to Cain. They also escorted Christ to Heaven at his Ascension. They are the angels most responsible for working miracles on earth, suspending the normal laws of nature when necessary. They also inspire mortals with grace and courage when they most need it.

Virtues ensure the stars and planets keep to their set courses, and also preside over the weather. They are in fact the planetary 'gods' of astrology. The Gnostics acknowledged that there was some truth in astrology but believed it could be overridden by faith in Christ. That all the main archangels are also rulers of the virtues fits the Neoplatonic scheme of them being the central choir of the central triad of the hierarchy. That is to say, they most nearly combine in themselves the qualities of all the other angels.

Ruling princes of the virtues are Michael, Gabriel, Raphael, Uriel, Anael, Zadkiel, Cassiel and, before his fall, Satan.

Dominions (Dominations, Lordships or Hashmallim)

Like the principalities, the dominions are responsible for maintaining order in the heavens and, says Dionysius, are forever aspiring for complete harmony among the angelic ranks. Also known as the Lords or Kuriotetes, they rarely appear before humans. They govern creation on the physical plane and guard the laws of nature and the elements.

Dionysius says of these angels that, 'The revealing name "dominions" signifies in my view, a lifting up which is free, unfettered by earthly tendencies and uninclined towards any of those tyrannical qualities which characterize a harsh dominion ... it is above any abject creation of slaves.' The dominions characterize power without oppression, government that feels like liberation. They are the model of how to command others without them feeling diminished by it. Elsewhere he adds, 'they regulate angels' duties and are perpetually aspiring to true lordship; through them the majesty of God is manifested.'

Ruling princes of the dominions are Hashmal (or Chasmal, 'Fire-Speaking'), Zadkiel, Muriel, Zacharel and Yahriel.

FIRST TRIAD

Thrones (Ophanim)

The title of the most sublime and exalted thrones conveys that in them there is a transcendence over every earthly defect, as shown by their looking towards the ultimate heights. It conveys that they are forever separated from what is inferior, that they are completely intent upon remaining always and forever in the presence of Him who is truly the most high; free of all passion and material concern. They are utterly available to receive the divine visitation. They bear God and are ever open, like servants, to welcome God.

PSEUDO-DIONYSIUS: *THE CELESTIAL HIERARCHY*

Allowing for the element of confusion and overlapping of functions mentioned earlier, the thrones (ophanim or galgallin) appear to be the living chariots which the cherubim drive for God when he travels abroad through the universe. They are forever in his presence and singing his praises.

Ophanim are the strangest-looking of all the angels and are described by Ezekiel and others as having the appearance of great fiery wheels filled with eyes. They are the 'wheels of the Merkabah', the chariot of God. They are also (perhaps in another form) the impartial and humane administrators of divine justice on the level of the fourth (central) heaven. Ophanim are the mediators between the first and second triads and their hymns translate the love of the seraphim and the wisdom of the cherubim into a form comprehensible to the lesser angels. The court of the ophanim is where matters of divine justice are settled and the will of the Godhead made known to ministering angels.

'Behold, a whirlwind came out of the north, a great cloud, and a fire infolding itself, and a brightness was about it, and out of the midst thereof as the colour of amber, out of the midst of the fire. Also out of the midst thereof came the likeness of four living creatures. And this was their appearance; they had the likeness of a man. And every one had four faces, and every one had four wings. And their feet were straight feet; and the sole of their feet was like the sole of a calf's foot: and they sparkled like the colour of burnished brass. And they had the hands of a man under their wings on their four sides; and they four had their faces and their wings.

'Their wings were joined one to another; they turned not when they went; they went every one straight forward. As for the likeness of their faces, they four had the face of a man, and the face of a lion, on the right side: and they four had the face of an ox on the left side; they four also had the face of an eagle. Thus were their faces: and their wings were stretched upward; two wings of every one were joined one to another, and two covered their bodies. And they went every one straight forward: whither the spirit was to go, they went; and they turned not when they went.

'As for the likeness of the living creatures, their appearance was like burning coals of fire, and like the appearance of lamps: it went up and down among the living creatures; and the fire was bright, and out of the fire went forth lightning. And the living creatures ran and returned as the appearance of a flash of lightning.

'Now as I beheld the living creatures, behold one wheel upon the earth by the living creatures, with his four faces. The appearance of the wheels and their work was like unto the colour of a beryl: and they four had one likeness: and their appearance and their work was as it were a wheel in the middle of a wheel. When they went, they went upon their four sides: and they turned not when they went. As for their rings, they were so high that they were dreadful; and their rings were full of eyes round about them four. And when the living creatures went, the wheels went by them: and when the living creatures were lifted up from the earth, the wheels were lifted up. Whithersoever the spirit was to go, they went, thither was their spirit to go; and the wheels were lifted up over against them: for the spirit of the living creature was in the wheels. When those went, these went; and when those stood, these stood; and when those were lifted up from the earth, the wheels were lifted up over against them: for the spirit of the living creature was in the wheels.

'And the likeness of the firmament upon the heads of the living creature was as the colour of the terrible crystal, stretched forth over their heads above. And under the firmament were their wings straight, the one toward the other: every one had two, which covered on this side, and every one had two, which covered on that side, their bodies. And when they went, I heard the noise of their wings, like the noise of great waters, as the voice of the Almighty, the voice of speech, as the noise of an host: when they stood, they let down their wings. And there was a voice from the firmament that was over their heads, when they stood, and had let down their wings.

'And above the firmament that was over their heads was the likeness of a throne, as the appearance of a sapphire stone: and upon the likeness of the throne was the likeness as the appearance of a man above upon it. And I saw as the colour of amber, as the appearance of fire round about within it, from the appearance of his loins even upward, and from the appearance of his loins even downward, I saw as it were the appearance of fire, and it had brightness round about. As the appearance of the bow that is in the cloud in the day of rain, so was the appearance of the brightness round about. This was the appearance of the likeness of the glory of the Lord.'

Reading the first chapter of Ezekiel today, it is almost impossible not to think of flying saucers, thanks to Erich von Däniken and his successors since the 70s. Similarly, when reading about the Watchers in Genesis and Enoch it is now very easy to picture them as a party of 200 aliens settling in the mountains of Lebanon in around 35,000 BC. Many people now find this much easier than accepting a concept like the Celestial Hierarchy. The Watchers' activities do sound very much like genetic and sociological experiments being practised on their primitive humanoid neighbours, until their rulers decided they had gone too far and pulled the plug.

Some feel this diminishes the biblical legends but it does at least give a fresh angle on ideas and visions that might otherwise just have continued to gather dust in the further reaches of the Bible, which would be of interest only to committed believers. Thanks to von Däniken the passage from Ezekiel, and others, have been pored over by fresh generations. It demonstrates the power of myth to adapt itself to new circumstances, presenting its enigmatic message in new ways that force us to scratch our heads and think again.

Parallel universes are taking the place of the seven heavens and alien abduction is becoming more credible than being snatched up to heaven (or hell) by an angel. A defining characteristic of alien abduction is that it is almost impossible to prove it is not happening. On the other hand, many people are happy to accept the existence of angels and mystical experiences without any scientific or pseudo-scientific explanation. Possibly angels themselves do not care if they are perceived as aliens as long as their message gets across. Then again, it's possible that both angels and aliens exist at the same time, both taking an interest in our world from their own strange perspectives. Possibly neither exist, which leaves us to wonder why some imaginations are driven to create them.

Princes of the ophanim are Galgaliel, Raphael, Zaphkiel, Raziel, Oriphiel, and Jophiel.

Cherubim

> *The name cherubim signifies the power to know and see God, to receive the greatest gifts of his light, to contemplate the divine splendour in primordial power, to be filled with the gifts that bring wisdom and to share these generously with subordinates as a part of the beneficent outpouring of wisdom.*
>
> PSEUDO-DIONYSIUS: *THE CELESTIAL HIERARCHY*

The second highest choir of angels is that of the cherubim, of whom there are said to be six (though possibly these are just their princes). They are mentioned most often in the Old Testament because of their images being used to decorate the Ark of the

Covenant and Solomon's Temple. Sadly, no exact description is given of what they looked like, perhaps because it was assumed that people already knew.

The Ark of the Covenant contained the stone tablets of the Ten Commandments that Moses received on Mount Sinai, samples of the manna that fed the Jews in the wilderness and Aaron's rod. It served as a kind of mobile altar during the Israelites' wanderings in the desert after leaving Egypt. An impromptu temple was built around it whenever camp was made. On either side of the lid or 'Mercy Seat' of the Ark were two carved golden cherubim, between whose overarching wings the 'spirit of God' was said to dwell. It addressed Moses and a few select others directly and occasionally blasted those who were presumptuous to eternity. The two angels that greeted visitors to Christ's tomb after his resurrection seem a deliberate echo of this design.

When the Jews settled down and Solomon came to build his great Temple in Jerusalem, the motif of cherubim was repeated on a grander and more permanent scale carved out of olive wood. This is described in intense detail in several passages of the Old Testament (e.g. Exodus 25.18–22: 36.8; Numbers 7.89; I Kings 6.23: 7.29, 36). Apocryphal legend also says that the two great statues of cherubim in Solomon's Temple were in the habit of facing each other when God was pleased with his people, and turning to the wall when He was not.

And the cherubim shall stretch forth their wings on high, covering the mercy seat with their wings, and their faces shall look one to another.

EXODUS 25

Real live cherubim also played an active part in the Old Testament story. As we have seen, it was they who drove Adam and Eve out of Eden and guarded the entrance so they could not return. They were also personifications of the winds, God's charioteers when He moved abroad through the universe, as well as being His messengers and overseeing the government of the kingdom of heaven. As the middle rank of the highest triad they are most representative of the three highest orders and so, in this sense, it is justifiable to describe them as the 'highest angels', as they have been at times.

According to some, the name 'cherubim' means 'Fullness of Knowledge', though it is related to the Assyrian word 'karibu' meaning 'interceder' or 'one who prays'. In Babylon they were represented as winged sphinxes, massive carvings of which guarded the temple gates. The name is also said to mean 'to be near' because the cherubim were the immediate courtiers and guardians of divinity.

Many other Babylonian gods became either angels or demons, and many of their legends (such as those of the Tree of Life and the Deluge) were simply absorbed into Hebrew legend, more or less unchanged.

Besides being God's charioteers, messengers, and instruments of his will, cherubim in the Old Testament were God's record keepers and guardians of the sun, moon and stars, whose fixed progress through the heavens they ensured in their parallel role of virtues. Many have assumed that the strange four-headed creatures described in Ezekiel's vision, quoted above, are cherubim. If one turns to Chapter 10 of Ezekiel, there is every reason to accept this, but there is also a good case to be made for them being seraphim and, purely for convenience, that is what we shall do.

It does not actually make much difference because the lists of 'princes' of the cherubim are almost identical to those of the seraphim and both have been referred to in various places as 'the highest angelic order'. Dionysius distinguishes between them by saying that cherubim interpret the love of God while seraphim interpret his wisdom.

The princes of the Cherubim were Gabriel, Raphael, Uriel, Zophiel, Cherubiel and Satan before his Fall. Satan was originally their leader.

Seraphim

For the designation seraphim really teaches this – a perennial circling around the divine things, penetrating warmth, the overflowing heat of a movement which never falters and never fails, a capacity to stamp their own image on subordinates by arousing and uplifting in them to a like flame, the same warmth. It means also the power to purify by means of the lightning flash and the flame. It means the ability to hold unveiled and undiminished both the light they have and the illumination they give out. It means the capacity to push aside and to do away with every obscuring shadow.

PSEUDO-DIONYSIUS: *THE CELESTIAL HIERARCHY*

It is generally accepted that the Seraphim are the four (or seven) angels inhabiting the innermost circle around God's throne. Seraphim are often described as 'fiery serpents' or the 'kindlers of fire' because they are made of divine light. Next to God himself they are the least material beings and their purpose is to kindle and increase the flame of spirituality in all beings further removed than themselves from the Quintessence. In Gnostic tradition they are described as the first 'emanations' of the Divine Unity, the primal, active elements of creation. As such, they have intelligence and at least the potential to attain a state of independence from each other and their source, but any exercise of that independence leads to war and chaos.

In mystical theory the Light or Fire at the heart of creation represents the primal unity that existed before the universe came into being through its progressive splitting into elements and sub-elements. The aim of the unfolding drama of the universe is to return all of creation to that primal unity, by way of working through all its apparent conflicts. In Gnostic terms we each contain a spark of divine fire which seeks to be reunited with its source. So too do all the angels, but the further removed all beings are from the Fountain of Light, the less conscious they are of their identity with it and each other. This is where conflicts arise.

Seraphim, representing the first differentiation of the Divine Light into its four main constituents, are in a sense four different aspects of it and, when working in perfect harmony, are more or less indistinguishable from the Godhead itself. As individuals, though, they have distinct characteristics. This is why it makes sense that the seraphim should be the four four-headed beasts in Ezekiel's vision. As the first division of the Divine into its four basic elements they are as close as we can get to grasping a vision of something that itself has no form or characteristics, because it is the union of all opposites.

In Ezekiel's vision, the four beings each have four heads, but elsewhere they each have a single head, namely a human, lion, eagle and ox. These were assigned to the four gospel writers who enshrined the teachings of Jesus with their books. Matthew was assigned the lion, symbolizing earthly kingship and representing Christ as the Lion of Judah and rightful king of the Jews. The ox was the symbol of Mark, representing the Christian attitude of submission to adversity. Luke was assigned the human face while the eagle denoted John, the wild visionary who was enthralled by Jesus and later wrote the book of Revelation.

The seraphim's natural place is immediately surrounding the heavenly throne and endlessly chanting the Trisagion, the song that begins 'Holy, holy, holy'. They are actually mentioned only once in the Bible, in Isaiah, Chapter 6, which begins:

'In the year that king Uzziah died I saw also the Lord sitting upon a throne, high and lifted up, and his train filled the temple. Above it stood the seraphims: each one had six wings; with twain he covered his face, and with twain he covered his feet, and with twain he did fly. And one cried unto another, and said, Holy, holy, holy, is the Lord of hosts: the whole earth is full of his glory.'

The seraphim are said to be so dazzling that even the angels of the second heaven find it hard to look upon them directly. However, when necessary they can leave their stations (or at least project part of themselves to other levels) to enter other spheres and even our own world, veiling their appearance as necessary.

The prime function of seraphim is to act as conduits of Divine Love. They are the mediators between the unknowable divine unity and the universe that arose from its splitting into ever more complex sub-divisions. Their name also implies that they are healers through the channelling of that love; the syllable 'ser' implying 'higher being' and 'rapha' meaning 'healer'. Seraphim are thereby associated with the twin serpents on the caduceus (or staff) of Hermes, Mercury and Aesculepeus, which is an emblem of the medical profession. The archangel and seraph Raphael is particularly associated with Mercury, while his name means simply 'Healer of God'.

In *The Book of Enoch* there are just four seraphim around the throne but other traditions suggest these are merely the princes of a whole legion of them. Certainly many more than four names have been put forward for them. These include Michael, Gabriel, Raphael, Uriel, Seraphiel (possibly an invented name), Metatron, Nathanael, Jehoel and Satan before his fall. Some of these may be different names for the same being, while Metatron and Michael are both named in different sources as being the supreme seraph.

CHAPTER SIX

FALLEN ANGELS

*Energy is the only life ... and Reason is the bound
circumference of Energy.*

WILLIAM BLAKE, *THE MARRIAGE OF HEAVEN AND HELL*

There are at least three clear classes of fallen angel in the legends associated with the Bible. The most ancient are those who, immediately after creation, decided to go their own way. This was apparently because they were given free will and chose to exercise it instead of surrendering their will back to God, as was expected. They gradually drifted so far away from their angelic origins that many became the demons who plagued humankind long before Satan's fall from grace. Demons thus have basically the same nature as angels, but have just followed a different course. Some became pagan gods, who weren't necessarily good or bad but just independent from the angels who stayed on in heaven.

The second kind are the Watchers or Grigori mentioned briefly in Genesis Chapter 6 and at length in *The Book of Enoch*. These were angels sent to earth to supervise the development of the infant human race but they could not resist trying to hurry it along, teaching humans secrets for which they were apparently not ready. Not only that, they fell in love with women, procreated with them and produced a race of giants that soon threatened to destroy the world. In many ways the Watchers are equivalent to the titans of Greek myth who were overthrown by Zeus and the other Olympian deities. According to Enoch, most of the Watchers were banished after the Flood to the northern regions of the third heaven, to reflect in misery on their fall from grace. The Watchers do not figure in the standard hierarchy of angels but were probably from the choir of principalities.

> *He was cast out into the earth, and his angels were cast out with him.*
>
> REVELATION 12

Then come the angels who later rebelled with Satan, a third of all the hosts of heaven according to the book of Revelation (12.4). These became the princes of hell under Satan (or Lucifer), the greatest of all and chief adversary of Michael, who replaced him as God's favourite. Biblical scholars suggest this rebellion must have taken place somewhere between the last books of the Old Testament and those of the New (i.e. in the two or three centuries before Christ) because there is barely a mention in the Old Testament of Satan having been banished from heaven. Usually his job is simply to test the loyalty of God's people by placing temptation or trial in their way (Job 1.6–12).

As well as these three main defections, there are countless other ways by which the demons have swollen their ranks. For instance, the souls of the Watchers' gigantic offspring are believed to have become demons after they had killed each other off. Unlike angels, demons can breed with each other and are forever trying to seduce the bright angels to their side. This is possible because although angels surrender their free will to the service of the Almighty they can reclaim it and break away. Those most likely to do this are the angels who patrol the borders of hell, because of their direct contact with the enemy. As in any war the combatants tend to become alike and, conversely, it seems the bright angels also sometimes win devils over to their side.

THE WATCHERS

And it came to pass, when men began to multiply on the face of the earth, and daughters were born unto them, that the sons of God saw the daughters of men, that they were fair; and they took them wives of all which they chose... There were giants in the earth in those days; and also after that, when the sons of God came in unto the daughters of men, and they bare children to them, the same became mighty men which were of old, men of renown.

GENESIS 6

Genesis passes very briefly over the tale of the Watchers but *The Book of Enoch* (from Chapter 7 onwards) goes into much greater detail. It tells us that there were two hundred of these angels under the leadership of Samyaza, the guardian of Egypt (otherwise known as Mastema):

'It happened after the sons of men had multiplied in those days, that daughters were born to them, elegant and beautiful. And when the angels, the sons of heaven, beheld them, they became enamoured of them, saying to each other: "Come, let us select for ourselves wives from the progeny of men, and let us beget children..."

'Then they took wives, each choosing for himself; whom they began to approach, and with whom they cohabited; teaching them sorcery, incantations and the dividing of roots and trees [i.e. herbal medicine]. And the women conceiving brought forth giants, whose stature was each three hundred cubits. These devoured all which the labour of men produced; until it became impossible to feed them...

'Moreover Azazyel taught men to make swords, knives, shields, breastplates, the fabrication of mirrors, and the workmanship of bracelets and ornaments, the use of paint, the beautifying of the eyebrows, the use of stones of every valuable and select kind, and of all sorts of dyes, so that the world became altered... Amazarak taught all the sorcerers, and dividers of roots; Armers taught the solution of sorcery; Barkayal taught the observers of the stars; Akibeel taught signs; Tamiel taught astronomy; And Asradel taught the motion of the moon. And men, being destroyed, cried out; and their voice reached to heaven.'

Enoch goes on to tell how Michael, Gabriel, Raphael and Uriel heard the cries of human misery on earth and took their complaint to God, who decided to destroy His creation and start again. The angel Arsayalalyur (possibly Uriel) was despatched to warn Noah of the Flood and how to survive it. Gabriel was sent to incite war between the giants so they should destroy each other, and other angels rounded up and

I heard my sons, who shared my prison house
Moan in their sleep and beg a crust of bread.
DANTE, *THE DIVINE COMEDY*: 'INFERNO'

imprisoned the Watchers in the third hell. Enoch himself was sent to tell the Watchers of God's judgement, and how they would be forced to witness the destruction of their children and all they had created on earth. The Watchers begged Enoch to plead for mercy with God on their behalf and soon afterwards he was lifted to heaven on a visionary wind:

'I proceeded until I arrived at a wall built with stones of crystal. A vibrating flame surrounded it, which began to strike me with terror. Into this vibrating flame I entered and drew nigh to a spacious habitation built also with stones of crystal, and crystal likewise was the ground. Its roof had the appearance of agitated stars and flashes of lightning; and among them were cherubim of fire in a stormy sky. A flame burned around its walls and its portal blazed with fire.

'When I entered into this dwelling it was hot as fire and cold as ice... And behold there was another habitation more spacious than the former, every entrance to which was open before me, erected in the midst of a vibrating flame... Its floor was on fire; above were lightnings and agitated stars, while its roof exhibited a blazing fire. Attentively I surveyed it and saw that it contained an exalted throne; the appearance of which was like that of frost; while its circumference resembled the orb of the brilliant sun; and there was the voice of the cherubim. From underneath this mighty throne, rivers of flaming fire issued. To look upon it was impossible. One in great glory sat upon it whose robe was brighter than the sun and whiter than snow.'

God refused mercy on the Watchers. Afterwards Enoch was taken on a tour of the seven heavens by the archangels and learned many things which he wrote in his book, long supposed to be the first book ever written by a human. The main reason Christianity officially discarded it (while at the same time adopting most of what it said) is because many of the revelations were discomforting, in particular, the understanding that each level of heaven touched a portion of hell in the north where fallen angels, demons and the damned were confined. This was replaced by the idea of a totally separate, seven-tiered hell existing somewhere beneath the earth, as portrayed by Dante and others.

The Watchers also appear in the apocryphal *The Book of Jubilees*. It says of them:

'In Jared's day the angels of the Lord descended on the earth, those who are named the Watchers, that they should instruct the children of men, and that they should do judgement and uprightness on the earth. And in the eleventh jubilee Jared took to himself a wife, and her name was Baraka ... and she bare him a son in the fifth week, in the fourth year of the jubilee, and he called his name Enoch. And he was the first among men that are born on earth who learnt writing and knowledge and wisdom.

'He wrote down the signs of heaven according to the order of their months in a book, that men might know the seasons of the years according to the order of their separate months. And he was the first to write a testimony. And he testified to the sons of men among the generations of the earth, and recounted the weeks of the jubilees. And he made known to them the days of the years, and set in order the months and recounted the Sabbaths of the years as we made them known to him. And what was and what will be he saw in a vision of his sleep, as it will happen to the children of men throughout their generations until the day of judgement; he saw and understood everything, and wrote his testimony, and placed the testimony on earth for all.'

ʃATAN AND HIS ANGELS

The name Satan means simply 'adversary' and in the Old Testament it is more a job description like 'prosecutor' than a personal name. God's favourite angel had the task of putting temptation in the way of His creatures to test their loyalty, and was the leader of other angels known collectively as 'the satans'. There are varying accounts of how by Jesus' day he had become the irrevocable enemy of God and gained a capital letter to his name, but all agree that it was basically pride.

The apocryphal *The Life of Adam and Eve* (Chapters 11–16) tells the story this way:

And [Adam] *cried out and said: 'Woe unto thee, devil. Why dost thou attack us for no cause? What hast thou to do with us? What have we done to thee that thou shouldst pursue us with such craft? Why doth thy malice so assail us? Have we taken away thy glory and caused thee to lose honour? Why dost thou harry us, and persecute us to the death in wickedness and envy?*

And with a heavy sigh, the devil spake: 'O Adam! All my hostility, envy, and sorrow is for thee, since it is for thee that I have been expelled from my glory, which I possessed in the heavens in the midst of the angels and for thee was I cast out into the earth.'

Adam answered, 'What dost thou tell me? What harm have I done to thee, or what is my fault against thee? Seeing that thou hast received no harm or injury from us, why dost thou pursue us?'

The devil replied: 'Adam, what dost thou tell me? It is for thy sake that I have been hurled from that place. When thou wast formed, I was hurled out of the presence of God and banished from the company of the angels. When God blew into thee the breath of life and thy face and likeness was made in the image of God, Michael also brought thee and made us worship thee in the sight of God; and God the Lord spake: "Here is Adam. I have made him in our image and likeness."'

And Michael went out and called all the angels saying: 'Worship the image of God as the Lord God hath commanded.' And Michael himself worshipped first; then he called me and said: 'Worship the image of God the Lord.' And I answered: 'I have no need to worship Adam.' And since Michael kept urging me to worship, I said to him: 'Why dost thou urge me? I will not worship an inferior and younger being. I am his senior in the Creation, before he was made, I already was. It is his duty to worship me.'

When the angels who were under me heard this, they refused to worship him also. And Michael saith: 'Worship the image of God, but if thou wilt not worship him, the Lord God will be wrath with thee.'

And I said: 'If He be wrath with me, I will set my seat above the stars of heaven and will be like the Highest.'

And so God the Lord was wrath with me and banished me and my angels from our glory; and on thy account were we expelled from our abodes into this world and hurled onto the earth. And straightaway we were overcome with grief, since we had been spoiled of so great glory. And we were grieved when we saw thee in such joy and luxury. And with guile I cheated thy wife and caused thee to be expelled through her doing from thy joy and luxury, as I have been driven out of my glory.

Depart from me ye cursed, into everlasting fire, prepared for the devil and all his angels.
MATTHEW 25

Islam has a very similar tale about Iblis, its equivalent of Satan, whose name derives from the Arabic for 'despair'. Iblis is also called Sheitan, the generic name for demons, and is sometimes known as the 'father of the Sheitans'.

In the beginning, Iblis was one of the greatest angels and the favourite of God. But when God created Adam and told his angels to bow before him, Iblis refused, saying: 'Why should I who was created from divine fire, bow before this creature made from dust?' Allah cursed him and banished him from heaven, but relented to the extent that Iblis is allowed to wander the earth until the Day of Judgement.

In Islamic legend it was Iblis who tempted Eve, having persuaded the serpent to smuggle him into Eden in its mouth in return for three mystic words that would grant it immortality.

Other versions of this tale cast Satan in a more sympathetic light by saying the reason Satan refused to bow before Adam was that God had previously told his angels to bow to none but Himself, and later forgot this. So Satan was in fact being true to his maker. But the problem with either of these versions of events is that they place Satan's rebellion at the start of Creation whereas in the Bible he does not appear to have fallen till much later. What's quite possible is that the story tells of an earlier angel who fell at the creation of Adam and Eve, and who was later identified with, or absorbed into, the figure of Satan. This happened to many other archdemons. It might have been Asmodeus, who is often said to be the one who tempted Adam and Eve, and who also

appears in *The Book of Tobit*. More likely it was Beelzebub ('Lord of the Flies'), who was considered by many Jews in New Testament times to be the archdemon. This became simply another name for Satan but in Jesus' time they were seen as distinct beings. In *The Book of Jubilees* Satan is made subordinate to Beelzebub for a time, despite being inherently more powerful, in return for Beelzebub releasing the souls of the saints from the underworld.

Another name almost inseparable from Satan is Lucifer, who is mentioned just once in the Old Testament by Isaiah. The famous passage from Chapter 14 is often quoted as evidence that the heavenly rebellion happened in Isaiah's day:

'How art thou fallen from heaven, O Lucifer, son of the morning! How art thou cut down to the ground, which didst weaken the nations! For thou hast said in thine heart, I will ascend into heaven, I will exalt my throne above the stars of God. I will sit also upon the mount of the congregation, in the sides of the north: I will ascend above the heights of the clouds; I will be like the most High. Yet thou shalt be brought down to hell, to the sides of the pit. They that see thee shall narrowly look upon thee, and consider thee, saying, "Is this the man that made the earth to tremble, that did shake kingdoms?"'

This is often read as a description of Satan's fall but is far more likely to have simply predicted the fall of Babylon, with Lucifer as its guardian angel. But once the connection had been made between Lucifer and Satan, it stuck. Like Satan, Lucifer is said to have been the most glorious of angels before his fall, the Light-bringer, the Morning Star, herald of the dawn. This role was later taken over by Jesus himself, as he says in the book of Revelation: 'I am the root and the offspring of David, and the bright and morning star' (Revelation 22.16).

On the wilder shores of speculation this has led to suggestions that Lucifer and Jesus were identical, but this is like the even wilder speculation that there was once another major planet called Lucifer that was destroyed by a meteor and became the asteroid belt. An interesting notion if it could be proved, but rather unlikely. What is more likely is that Lucifer and Jesus were twinned in the same way that many bright and dark angels were. Or that Jesus, as he was preparing in heaven for the Incarnation, displaced Lucifer as the one closest to God, so jealousy and rebellion followed. The one thing everyone agrees on is that Satan (Lucifer) rebelled through pride. That is not to say that no evil existed before this. As we have seen, there were demons aplenty plaguing the world from the very beginning, but with the fall of Satan evil entered a new dimension of subtlety. Having been one of the highest angels, Satan understood the mind of God better than all other demons, who were gradually either absorbed into Satan or placed in command of his many legions.

*Through all the empyrean: down they fell
Driven headlong from the pitch of heaven.*
MILTON: *PARADISE LOST*

The Gnostic Christians shared most of these ideas about fallen angels but often reached surprisingly different conclusions. Many believed that Jehovah himself was a fallen angel or archon named Ialdabaoth who falsely claimed to be the Supreme Being and stole all the glory of Creation for himself. Also known as the Demiurge and the Usurper, Ialdabaoth was believed to have tricked the Jews into thinking him the supreme and perfectly good God, despite occasionally giving way to jealous rages and breaking most of his own Commandments.

It now seems obvious why the Gnostics were branded heretics and persecuted to extinction by the fifth century, but it was touch and go for a while whether Gnostic or Pauline Christianity would prevail. In the end the greater discipline and political muscle of Paul's Roman Church won the day. The problem with the Gnostics was that they took what Jesus said about inspiration from the Holy Ghost literally and saw no reason against producing more and more gospels and revelations. Some were widely accepted but others led the Gnostics to splinter into countless bickering sects that were no match for a Roman Church that had decided to cut off the supply of fresh scriptures once and for all. For ages Gnostic beliefs were only known through the slanted arguments of their enemies but the balance has been redressed a little in the last century or so by finds of manuscript hoards such as that at Nag Hammadi. Among other treasures they include the priceless *Pistis Sophia*, the most famous and influential of the Gnostic scriptures.

The Gnostics saw the Great Mother Sophia as the originator of all life, the mother of Jehovah as much as Mary was the mother of Jesus. Great Mother Sophia was equal to, or one half of, God and because of this Gnostic women enjoyed equal status with men and produced many famous prophetesses, chief of whom was Mary Magdalene, who was also called Pistis Sophia Prunikos (meaning 'Faith Wisdom Whore').

Sophia actually emerged from another Divine Being named Abraxas, who was both male and female. Abraxas also produced other 'emanations', divine beings with abstract names such as Love, Power, Compassion, Grace, Mercy, Thought and Truth. Sophia and the others generated still more emanations or aeons who built up a hierarchy resembling that of the angels, except that they were male and female and had only seven ranks, each corresponding to one of the heavens. These were most commonly titled Ancient Ones, Powers, Thrones, Dominions, Authorities, Lesser Gods and Rulers.

In time, these Aeons grew conscious of their own being and then God (or Abraxas) withdrew, leaving them to work out their own destinies and find their own way back to the Source. This led to rebellion among the angels, one third of whom left heaven and came down to our world of space and time, making their home here as archons. They were said to be the pagan planetary gods who ruled our world through the laws of astrology. When Jesus died he is said to have visited their sphere and disrupted the workings of astrology, so that any true Christian became immune to both astrology and the archons.

One of the most famous Gnostics was Simon Magus, who was said to travel around with a reformed prostitute claiming to be the reincarnation of Helen of Troy. Under the supposed authorship of Simon Magus some Gnostic ideas survived into the Middle Ages and beyond in esoteric and occult circles. Some claim to have traced a direct line of evolution from Gnosticism to alchemy, Rosicrucianism and nineteenth-century theosophy, with many exotic philosophical offshoots along the way. The more obscure writings of William Blake are steeped in Gnostic belief, particularly the idea of Jehovah being Satan in disguise, which might have shocked the Victorians, who adopted his hymn 'Jerusalem' as their second national anthem. Luckily, the sheer obscurity of Blake's 'prophetic' writings kept people from noticing.

The names and guises of the fallen angels are as various as those of their enemies, the bright angels who try to steer us towards enlightenment. Many earlier devils were simply absorbed into the figure of Satan once he became the arch-enemy of heaven;

their names simply became colourful alternatives. But it is perhaps worth looking at some of those who seemed to have once had distinct identities.

Beelzebub

In the Gospels Beelzebub is often referred to as the 'Prince of Demons', implying that it is just another name for Satan, but until the Middle Ages they were seen as quite distinct. The apocryphal *The Gospel of Nicodemus* tells of Jesus promoting Beelzebub over Satan for not opposing his rescue of the saints from hell after his Crucifixion.

Beelzebub was originally a Philistine deity (the god *baal* or *beel* of Zebub, near Ekron, just west of Jerusalem). He only appears in the Old Testament in connection with the death of King Ahaziah, who ruled the Israelites in the days of Elijah. Ahaziah had turned away from Jehovah to the worship of Baal, a collective name for various Philistine gods generally worshipped on hilltops. The first chapter of the second book of Kings describes how Ahaziah fell from a roof. From his sickbed he sent a messenger to ask Beelzebub (or his oracle) if he would recover. An angel sent Elijah to intercept the messenger and send him back to the

king with a warning that because he did not worship the true god he would surely die where he lay. The king then sent a captain and fifty men but when they met Elijah he called down fire from heaven and destroyed them all. The king sent a second troop that met the same fate. The third captain pleaded with Elijah for mercy, so Elijah returned with him to the king and delivered his message in person. Ahaziah, still not repenting, duly died in his bed.

In this story Beelzebub could be seen as just a powerful local deity, the counterpart of a principality. How he rose to be considered Prince of the Demons is unknown but it may have followed from his closeness to Jerusalem, and from the king preferring him to Jehovah and treating them on an equal level. Beelzebub was also called 'Lord of the Flies' because of the swarms that hung around his bloodstained altar.

The Testament of Solomon tells how the wise king enslaved Beelzebub for a while. It happened like this: while Solomon was building his temple he noticed one of his favourite workers pining away. When asked about his trouble the man said that he was being visited nightly by a vampire demon who was draining his life by sucking blood from his thumb. Solomon prayed for guidance and after three days the archangel Raphael appeared and gave him a ring of power whose gem was engraved with a five-pointed star enclosing the unspoken name of God. This was the famous 'Seal of Solomon'. Solomon gave the ring to his worker with instructions from the angel and when the demon Ornias came for his nightly sup of blood, he was enslaved.

Solomon then sent his new slave to visit Beelzebub and enslave him with the ring too, setting him to work sawing blocks of marble for the temple. Having the Prince of Demons put to work like this soon attracted others, whom Solomon enslaved one by one, and the building work flew ahead, becoming one of the wonders of the ancient world.

Beelzebub was also the demon in whose name his enemies accused Jesus of casting out devils.

Belial

Belial is also often equated with Satan but seems distinct. In the Old Testament the word is often used as a general term for worthlessness, destruction or 'the abyss' (Sheol). But Belial also became personified as a Prince of Hell and of demons, sometimes as Beelzebub's lieutenant and sometimes as his lord. Solomon is said to have made Belial dance for his pleasure after enslaving him. In *The Gospel of Bartholomew*, Belial claims that he was once called Satan, the first angel created before Michael, Gabriel, Uriel, Raphael and all the rest. In several other apocryphal scriptures Belial is called Prince of this World and the future Antichrist. St Paul also seems to have thought that Belial and Satan were identical and the Roman Emperor Nero was believed by Christians at the time to be his incarnation. Milton, however, makes them distinct in *Paradise Lost*.

Belphegor

Another demon whose name derives from Baal (the Baal of Mt Phegor), Belphegor is the lewdest of demons and was once a Moabite god of fertility whose followers held orgies to increase the yield of their herds and crops.

The wandering Israelites are said in Numbers (Chapter 25) to have met the cult at Settim, their last stop before entering the land of Canaan. Many were tempted into joining these orgies, which so infuriated Jehovah that he ordered Moses to have them all (some 24,000) beheaded and then waged war on the tempters. The cult seems to have survived into the second century, however, and was tolerated by the Romans.

Before falling from grace, Belphegor is believed to have been a principality – and still has a tendency that way – as by popular tradition he has adopted France as his home. Belphegor often appears as a beautiful young woman and is closely related to the pagan Greek Priapus and Hindu Rutrem, both great champions of lust.

Mephistopheles

Mephistophiel or Mephistopheles' name means literally 'he who destroys by lies'. He is one of the seven main princes of hell and dark twin of Zadkiel, the angel of Jupiter. He has occasionally been confused with Satan but is usually accepted as a lieutenant. Sardonic, cynical, clever and seductive, he has been a favourite subject of literature and drama since the Middle Ages, thanks to the famous tale of his pact with Dr Faust. Like Satan in the book of Job, he appears to have a special pass to occasionally visit heaven for duels of wits with the angels.

Where Belphegor uses sensuality to lure people into damnation, Mephistopheles uses subtle argument, which is perhaps more dangerous. After all, history is full of well-meaning intellectuals whose work has been misinterpreted, resulting in mass destruction and misery. In fact, it is possible to argue that people who are convinced they are on the side of the angels cause most of the humanly inflicted grief in the world, while all along Mephistopheles is laughing in the wings. That is why Goethe allowed his Faust's soul to be rescued by angels at the end. His only real sin was reckless curiosity.

Samael

In Rabbinic literature Samael is considered 'chief of the satans' or Satan himself. Confusingly he is the namesake or twin of the angel Samael who rules the fifth heaven with a company of two million angels and is one of the seven 'Regents of the Earth'. He was Esau's guardian angel and principality of Edom.

Both Samaels are angels of death and it is often unclear which of them is at work and whether they have come to lead the soul to heaven or hell. God sent the bright Samael to fetch Moses' soul to heaven.

The devilish Samael is described as a serpent with twelve wings who tempted Eve in the Garden and fathered Cain on her. He is also said to have seduced Adam's first wife, Lilith, and fathered on her hordes of little demons. When God sent his angels to destroy them, she took her revenge by preying on the newborn of Adam's descendants in the form of a screech-owl or succubus.

At least one of their children survived, though, namely Asmodeus. Asmodeus was the demon whom Tobit had to overcome to enjoy his bride, and who mischievously made Noah drunk. He was originally a Persian moon deity skilled in mathematics and divining the future. He is the demon of gambling and other forms of entertainment, which he uses to try and lure people into sin. The angel Raphael is supposed to have banished him to Upper Egypt but he later escaped.

We could go on indefinitely with demons as there are almost as many demons in the

lists as angels, and they're just as fascinating. We could say more about Mastema, for instance, Egypt's guardian angel turned demon. He seems to have had a similar role to the Old Testament Satan in being a 'demon of adversity', who is tolerated by God because adversity often brings out true character and worth. It is said that God lent him a tenth of the devils being consigned to hell to carry out this work. Then there is Moloch, a demon with no obvious redeeming features, who demanded the sacrifice of children on his altars. There's also Nisroch, a relatively harmless eagle-headed devil whose main occupation appears to have been as head chef and bottle-washer in the underworld! But while the fallen angels are endlessly fascinating, they should not eclipse all the bright angels, so let's leave them there.

CONCLUSION

The interesting thing about angels is that once you look beyond the Bible there is a wealth of information about them. Much is contradictory and one can easily get lost in lists of names and attributes. What is more remarkable is the broad agreement of angelic lore across many cultures and how this has managed to persist for millennia, despite the many attempts to diminish it.

This broad picture is what we have aimed to capture. Readers whose appetites have been whetted for more can go to the original sources mentioned throughout this book, which these days are easier to find than ever before. Quotes from *The Book of Enoch* are taken from an old copy I happen to have. It reads well but there are other, possibly better translations to be found free on the Internet. Pseudo-Dionysius is rarer, but the Paulist Press in New York publishes a great translation by Colm Luibheid.

Most of the other apocryphal scriptures mentioned, such as the *The Book of Jubilees*, *The Gospel of Nicodemus* and several different *The Lives of Adam and Eve*, can also be found and make fascinating reading. That's the wonder of the Internet. It's our newest medium but it's already the best place to find ancient literature, unless you already happen to live near some great library. These days anyone with a computer in Timbuktu or Alice Springs can join the game.

It really is as revolutionary as the invention of printing, because again more and more people are free to go to original texts and make up their own minds about them. We often forget that neither Jesus nor his immediate disciples chose what went into the Bible, or even the New Testament. That was decided much later by committees whose aims were often more political than spiritual. It was also often touch and go which scriptures were excluded. Revelation was just one of many apocalyptic visions circulating at the time that were taken almost as seriously. Others were only just left out but still had a vast influence on the growth of our spiritual beliefs and are treasure troves of angelic lore.

This lore is not essential to an appreciation of angels. Many people are angel enthusiasts and believers, while knowing nothing of their background or history. Many want to know no more than they learn from immediate experience. Angels rarely seem to have taken much trouble to introduce or explain themselves; they usually just bear a timely message or inspiration. They have appeared to people of all faiths and none, to those who believe in them and those who don't. The need of the moment seems to be all that counts and so, if anything, they are more likely to appear to sinners than saints. Like Jesus, they also show

little regard for rank, reputation or any of the things we often take as measures of virtue. Each individual seems equally important to them.

Then there are the visionaries to whom angels have been such an everyday reality that they have never even thought to question their existence. People such as Caedmon, the illiterate bard of the Anglo Saxons and William Blake, who died happily at the age of three score and ten, singing hymns and praising the choirs of angels he saw gathering around his bed to take him finally to the paradise he had so often tried to describe.

Lives are still transformed by how people listen to their inner promptings, which can be seen as the voices or influence of angels. The brightest palace can become hell to those who have made the wrong choices. The grimmest slum can be paradise to those who are happy with who they are. Happiness and a sense of fulfilment are abstract, spiritual qualities, whether or not life is part of any grander scheme. So, in an everyday, secular sense, it remains true that following the prompting of our inner angel can lead to heaven. Usually it is less dramatic than that, but we've all had moments when the voice of conscience or temptation has suddenly felt loud, insistent and uncomfortably *other* than us, just as first romance reveals sudden new depths to all the love songs we have heard. Whether or not we are believers, angels are the embodiment of a brighter, kinder existence to which everyone can aspire.

Pictures courtesy of the Bridgeman Art Library, additional credits listed below:

Cover, 7 Sir Edward Burne-Jones, *Angel*;
2 Fra (Guido di Pietro) Angelico, *Adoration of an Angel* (panel);
3 Tommaso di Stefano Lunetti, *The Adoration of the Shepherds*, Christie's Images, London, UK;
4 & 68 Pietro Perugino, *The Agony in the Garden*, (detail);
5 & 40 John Melhuish Strudwick, *Angel*;
6 (t) & 94 (t) Juste de Gand, *The Last Supper* (detail);
6 (b) Egyptian Tapestry, Victoria & Albert Museum, London, UK;
8 (t) Giotto di Bondone, *Angels, from the Crucifixion* (detail);
8 (b) Phoebe Anna Traquair, *The Awakening*;
9 Vincent van Gogh, *Head of an Angel, after Rembrandt*;
10–11 Andrea Mantegna, *Putti with Butterfly Wings from the Camera degli Sposa*;
12 (tr) from the *Nuremberg Bible*;
12 (bl) Filippo di Matteo Torelli, *Missal 515*;
13 Jean-Honore Fragonard, *Swarm of Cupids* (*L'Essaim d'Amours*) Louvre, Paris, France/Giraudon;
14 Fra (Baccio della Porta) Bartolommeo, *The Mystic Marriage of St Catherine of Siena with Saints* (detail), Louvre, Paris, France/Peter Willi;
14 (b) & 15 (tl & br) Giovanni Baglione, *Studies of Putti*, Richard Philp, London, UK;
15 (cr) Raphael, *Putti* (detail from the Sistine Madonna);
16–17 Raphael, *Galatea* (detail of putto and dolphins);
18 (t) Dante Gabriel Rossetti, *Study for the head of a child angel in 'The Blessed Damozel'*, Mallett Gallery, London, UK;
18 (b) Jacques de Stella, *Christ Served by the Angels* (detail);
19 Giovanni Battista Rosso Fiorentino, *Two Cherubs Reading*, detail from *Madonna and Child with Saints*;
20–21 Gabriele Smargiassi, *The Death of Federigo da Montefeltro, Duke of Urbino*;
22 P.J. Crook, *The Guardian*, © Courtesy of Theo Waddington Fine Art;
23 Giovanni Segantini, *The Angel of Life*;
24 Francesco Botticini, *Tobias and the Archangel Raphael*;
26 (tl) Giovanni Battista Rosso Fiorentino, *Angel Playing the Lute*;
26 (br) Guariento de Arpo, *Archangel Michael*;
27 *Angeli Laudantes* tapestry designed by Henry Dearle, orig. drawn by Edward Burne-Jones;
28 (l) Hans Memling, *The Archangel Michael*, from a triptych, Christie's Images, London, UK;
29 Dirck Bouts, *Paradise of the Symbolic Fountain*;
31 Arthur Hacker, *The Cloister or the World*, Bradford Art Galleries and Museums, West Yorkshire, UK;
32 Domenico di Michelino, *Dante Reading from 'The Divine Comedy'*;
33 Paolo Caliari Veronese, *The Eternal Father*;
34–35 Nicolaes Pietersz Berchem, *The Annunciation to the Shepherds*, Bristol City Museum and Art Gallery, UK;
36 (t) detail from Nicolaes Pietersz Berchem, *The Annunciation to the Shepherds*, Bristol City Museum and Art Gallery, UK;
36 (br) & 37 Juan Correa, *The Nativity*;
38 Melozzo da Forli, *The Annunciating Angel Gabriel*;
39 Neri di Bicci, *The Annunciation*;
41 Pietro Perugino, *Vallombrosa Altarpiece*;
43 Lexden L. Pocock, *Inspiration of Caedmon*, Cheltenham Art Gallery and Museums, Gloucestershire, UK;
44 Paul Baudry, *The Dream of St Cecilia*;
45 *Christmas Greetings*, 1950s Christmas card;
46–47 Jean Theodore Dupas, *Angels of Peace*, Giraudon/BAL;
48 Icon of the Angel Michael;

49 Greek School, *Abraham and the Three Angels*, Richardson and Kailas Icons, London, UK;
51 Catalan Master, *St Michael Vanquishing Evil*, Phillips, The International Fine Art Auctioneers;
52 (bl) Fra (Guido di Pietro) Angelico, *The Annunciation* (detail);
52–53 George William Joy, *Joan of Arc Asleep*;
54 Francesco Ubertini Verdi Bachiacca, *Tobias and the Angel*;
55 William Blake, *Jacob's Ladder*;
57 Carlos Schwabe, *The Angel of Death*, Palais de Tokyo, Paris, France/Peter Willi;
58 (b) Jacopo Pontormo, *The Annunciation*, Capponi Chapel, Santa Felicita, Florence, Italy/Peter Willi;
59 Anonymous, *Archangel Azrael with a Gun*;
60–61 John Melhuish Strudwick, *The Ramparts of God's House*, Christie's Images, London, UK;
62 Giovanni di Paolo di Grazia, *Five Angels Dancing Before the Sun*, Musée Conde, Chantilly, France/Lauros-Giraudon;
63 Benozzo di Lese di Sandro Gozzoli, *Angels in a Heavenly Landscape*, from *The Journey of the Magi*;
64 Hubert Robert, *Spirit of the Tomb*;
65 George Richmond, *The Agony in the Garden*, Yale Center for British Art, Paul Mellon Collection, USA;
65 (b) 16th-Century Astrological Chart, *Portolan Map*, Lambeth Palace Library, London, UK;
67 Northern School, Russian Icon of the Prophet Elijah, Mark Gallery, London, UK;
67 (b) Gustave Doré, *Beatrice Ascends with Dante to the Planet Mercury*;
detail 66, 69, detail 70, detail 73: Pietro Perugino, *The Ascension of Christ*, Musée des Beaux-Arts, Lyons, France/Peter Willi;
71 William Blake, *Christ in the Sepulchre, Guarded by Angels*;
72 Fra (Guido di Pietro) Angelico, *Christ Glorified in the Court of Heaven*;
73 Matthias Grunewald, *Concert of Angels* from the Isenheim Altarpiece, Giraudon;
74 Evelyn de Morgan, *The Light Shineth in Darkness and the Darkness Comprehendeth it Not*, The Morgan Foundation, London, UK;
76–77 William Blake, *Good and Evil Angels Struggling for the Possession of a Child*, Cecil Higgins Art Gallery, Bedford, Bedfordshire, UK;
79 Luca Giordano, *Archangel Michael Overthrows the Rebel Angel*;
80 Byzantine icon of Archangels Michael and Gabriel, Richardson and Kailas Icons, London, UK;
81 William Blake, *Count Ugolino and his Sons in Prison: Illustration for 'Inferno', canto 33*, Fitzwilliam Museum, University of Cambridge, UK;
82 & 92 Ferdinand Victor Eugene Delacroix, *Mephistopheles' Prologue in the Sky* from Goethe's *Faust*;
83 Marco D'Oggiono, *The Archangels Triumphing Over Lucifer*;
84 Francis Danby, *Apocalypse*;
85 William Blake, *Satan Arousing the Rebel Angels*;
86–87 Luca Signorelli, *Devils*, from *The Last Judgement* (detail);
88 *The Angel of Death* (vellum);
88 (b) Julio de Mantua, *Heaven and Hell* engraved by Hieronymus Cock;
89 Gustave Doré, (after), *Satan and Beelzebub*, engraved by Charles Laplante;
91 Evelyn de Morgan, *The Angel of Death*, The de Morgan Foundation, London, UK;
93 Hugo Simberg, *Wounded Angel*, Museum of Finnish Art, Ateneum, Helsinki, Finland;

Image courtesy of Gateshead Council: 95 Photograph by Keith Paisley, *Angel of the North*, Sculpture by Antony Gormley.